Rachel Turner is Family Life ████████████████
Previous roles include full-ti ████████████████
*and National Children's Work Coordinator for New Wine. She
continues to consult, speak at conferences and run training days for
parents, children and youth workers around the UK and Europe.*

Barnabas
for
Children

Text copyright © Rachel Turner 2015
The author asserts the moral right to be identified as the author of this work

Published by
The Bible Reading Fellowship
15 The Chambers, Vineyard
Abingdon OX14 3FE
United Kingdom
Tel: +44 (0)1865 319700
Email: enquiries@brf.org.uk
Website: www.brf.org.uk
BRF is a Registered Charity

ISBN 978 0 85746 167 4
First published 2015
10 9 8 7 6 5 4 3 2 1 0
All rights reserved

Acknowledgements
Unless otherwise stated, scripture quotations are taken from The Holy Bible, New International Version (Anglicised edition) copyright © 1979, 1984, 2011 by Biblica. Used by permission of Hodder & Stoughton Publishers, an Hachette UK company. All rights reserved. NIV is a registered trademark of Biblica. UK trademark number 1448790.

Scripture taken from the New Century Version®. Copyright © 2005 by Thomas Nelson. Used by permission. All rights reserved.

Cover photo: Lightstock

Every effort has been made to trace and contact copyright owners for material used in this resource. We apologise for any inadvertent omissions or errors, and would ask those concerned to contact us so that full acknowledgement can be made in the future.

A catalogue record for this book is available from the British Library

Printed and bound by CPI Group (UK) Ltd, Croydon CR0 4YY

Parenting children

for a life of confidence

Releasing children to live in God's strength

Rachel Turner

For my husband, Mark, who anchors me in all ways

Acknowledgements

Caleb Turner: I can never truly describe the joy it is to be your mother. Thank you for your endless grace, your encouragements and cheers, and for always playing with me when I ask. I'm so grateful that I get to laugh and share hearts with you every day.

My husband: without you I would have starved to death and gone crazy on this journey. Thank you for your steadfastness in the face of my creative process, passionate rants, and flops.

My mother, Susan Hart: thank you for your constant wisdom, your faithfulness and your firm belief that this book would actually come together. I am deeply humbled to be your daughter.

My dad, Terry Hart: thank you for a lifetime of love, laughter and togetherness. So much of who I am can be traced to your letting me experiment and learn random skills with you.

My editor, Olivia Warburton: thank you for your mercy and grace and for sticking with me as I tried to sift this book out of my brain. I am very grateful for you in my life.

To my church, St Paul's Hammersmith: thank you for welcoming me into the heart of your community. I have felt so blessed to be held in such a tight, committed family and team.

Thank you to all my friends who encouraged me and supported our family while I wrote: Elaine Webster, Elle Bird, Will Leaf, Annie and Pete Willmot, Nick and Becky Drake, Fiona East, David and Brittney Withers, Liz Baddaley and Jill Andrews, Katherine Message, Matt Read, Josh Lees and Rachel Norburn.

Contents

Chapter 1: Core of confidence 7

Section 1: Foundations

Chapter 2: It's not about me 19

Chapter 3: I'm not finished yet...31

Section 2: Key tools

Chapter 4: Introduction of hearts and minds...........................41

Chapter 5: Hearts..45

Chapter 6: Minds..57

Section 3: Everyday applications

Chapter 7: Introduction to everyday applications...................69

Chapter 8: Embrace the journey: who am I? 73

Chapter 9: Encouraging for confidence 85

Chapter 10: Media and the world's messages........................95

Chapter 11: Comparison and contentment 119

Chapter 12: Manliness and beauty 131

Chapter 13: Comparison and humility.................................. 141

Chapter 14: Failure.. 161

Chapter 15: Friendships and peer pressure.......................... 175

Conclusion 190

Notes... 191

*

— Chapter 1 —

Core of confidence

Scripture is full of people who just ooze confidence. Moses and Aaron strolled into Pharaoh's palace to declare God's purpose and said, 'Let my people go!' Jeremiah delivered God's words to kings and rulers with not an eyebrow flicker of doubt. Jesus challenged smug religious leaders and calmly dealt with violent mobs. Young Mary stood boldly under the judgement of her community because she had a deep knowledge of her call. Paul weathered imprisonment and shipwrecks without fear or worry.

If you have ever been around someone who is truly confident, you will find it strangely compelling. The blend of openness, genuineness and freedom is so appealing. In our society, confidence is not just a quality to be prized; it is a commodity to be greatly treasured. Confidence roots us in who we are and enables us to deal with anything and everything with strength and peace. It is the essence of a 'can-do' approach. We want it for ourselves and we want it for our children.

The world has a formula for confidence. It goes like this:

You are amazing and perfect, just the way you are. People should love and accept you for who you are, and, if they don't, well, that's their problem. Be proud of yourself! Change for no one! Love yourself wholeheartedly! Figure out who you are, and then shout it from the rooftops: 'My name is Rachel Turner and I AM AWESOME!'

Some of the Christian community goes along with this formula. We can be told in church:

God made you perfect and precious. You are unique and wonderful, like a gemstone in his eyes, worthy of so much. To criticise yourself is to criticise your creator, so stand up tall, look in the mirror and say, 'I am perfect just the way I am! I have distinctive talents and spiritual gifts that only I can bring to the world. I can do all things through Christ who gives me strength. Bring it on! I am special, important, and I AM AWESOME!'

We think that if our children could just believe those statements deep in their hearts, then they would be confident. If they could discover who they are and express it well, then they would have joy. If only they could live those beliefs, they would be able to weather the storms in the world.

The problem is that the formula doesn't work. Our children are still swayed by the latest trends at school, and they want the toys that everybody else wants. They are still self-conscious about their voices or their clothes or their bodies. They still get random fears, and they still buckle under performance pressure. We see their confidence being slowly torn away and self-doubt creeping in, so we repeat the mantra again and again to them: 'You are perfect just the way you are. You are unique. You are special. You are awesome.' But what we long for most for our children—the inner strength of true long-lasting confidence—rarely, if ever, emerges in them.

The reason, I believe, is that we have a wrong view of confidence.

I don't think Moses successfully led a nation because he strongly believed in his unique talents. I don't think Samuel was confident because he looked in the mirror and truly believed, 'I am special. I am unique. I am perfect just the way I am.' I don't think Paul sang in prison with joy because he loved expressing his true inner self and had a great singing voice. I don't think Mary was bold, after hearing from the angel that she was to be the mother of the Son of God, because she daily reminded herself, 'I am awesome!'

Do you think their confidence came from their own opinions of themselves? Of course not. So, since we hold up these people in scripture as some of the most confident, effective, peaceful champions of faith and life, we need to ask ourselves: what was their secret?

Their core of confidence was different. Their core of confidence was in God, and not in themselves. When people in the Bible speak of confidence, they are almost universally referring to a confidence in God, not a confidence in themselves. As one of the psalmists says, 'For you have been my hope, Sovereign Lord, my confidence since my youth' (Psalm 71:5; for other examples, see Jeremiah 17:7; 2 Corinthians 3:1–6; Ephesians 3:12).

Look at people in the Bible. What if King Hezekiah and the judge Deborah were so confident because they were aware that their success really wasn't about their capability at all? What if the apostle John was so confident because he knew he was fully and totally loved by a faithful God, imperfect as he was? What if Peter was so confident because he knew that God's grace was perfect in all his weaknesses, and that God wasn't finished with him yet? What if Elizabeth's joy and confidence were rooted in the humble knowledge that God was inviting her, as the mother of John the Baptist, to be a small part of his mind-blowing salvation plan?

What would our children's confidence look like if they truly knew how good and perfect and wonderful God is, and if they knew in every part of themselves that his love is very real and he is deeply faithful? What would our children do and how much joy would they have if they were content with being imperfect and were unimpressed by the world's expectations? What would their days be like if they could walk into school thinking, 'God, what shall we do together today?' instead of 'Please, God, I just want people to like me'?

I think that confidence, essentially, is about freedom— freedom to just be in the place where I am, unafraid, totally loved by God, doing what he is asking me to do, and enjoying loving him and the community I am in. In this book we are going to explore how to develop this core of confidence in our children's lives.

I believe that a healthy core of confidence consists of these three beliefs, which underpin all the tools and skills that we will be building through this book:

- God is awesome and holy, and he loves me totally and unreasonably.
- God is daily shaping me to be more like him, and I am not finished yet.
- I am invited to be a small part of God's wonderful plans.

I want to say a few things to you before we begin. First of all, God is awesome and holy and he loves *you* beyond anything you could ever imagine. He is daily shaping you, as an individual and as a parent, to be more like him, and he isn't finished with you yet. He is calling you to be a small part of his body to accomplish his wonderful plans and purposes on this earth, and that includes his marvellous plans for your child to be solidly confident, free, loved and rooted in him. You are not alone.

Effective spiritual parenting isn't a destination to reach or a mountain to climb. No one ever wakes up one morning and declares that they are an awesome parent. No one ever stands up and says, 'Yes, I am exactly the parent I want to be. I know how to handle every situation with each and every one of my children. I have no doubts about my approach or my decisions, and I consistently deliver as the ultimate parent. I can now put a big "tick" next to those skills and finally give my attention to other things.' Parenting is a journey. It is a dance. It's a constant adjustment to ever-changing human beings and a daily process of learning and failing and succeeding. It's a joy and a worry, a delight and an agony. It's a life's call that doesn't end when our children move out. Parenting continues.

God designed it that way. He has placed your children in your particular home and under your influence. Whether they came into your family through birth, adoption, fostering or some other unexpected circumstance, God has asked you to parent these children spiritually, physically, emotionally and mentally. The combination of their personalities and your parenting is going to shape them into the adults they will become, and you have no guarantees about what their adulthood will look like. You can only do your part—the part God asks you to do.

At the core of our call as parents, at the very root of our place in our children's lives, is the call from God to nurture their lifelong spiritual walk with him, to raise them to be connected to the one from whom all love, healing, joy, peace and freedom flow. This call is designed to be one of our deepest joys.

When we first begin to think about parenting for confidence, we may think about all the time it will require and all the help we need—from home devotionals, Bibles, books, CDs, DVDs, experts and churches. However, it's not about the paraphernalia or schedules or formulas or programmes. It's about positioning.

God placed us exactly where we need to be in order to shape our children spiritually, right in the thick of the ordinary, everyday, mundane patterns of life. Deuteronomy 6:5–9 says:

Love the Lord your God with all your heart and with all your soul and with all your strength. These commandments that I give you today are to be on your hearts. Impress them on your children. Talk about them when you sit at home and when you walk along the road, when you lie down and when you get up. Tie them as symbols on your hands and bind them on your foreheads. Write them on the door-frames of your houses and on your gates.

It's in the ordinary moments that we can shape our children spiritually. It's in the little bits of time as we walk along the road or as we brush our teeth or as we read books together. You were placed by God in the run-of-the-mill, ordinary realm of life alongside your children because it is the most powerful and most influential place to be.

I am a tired and busy parent, just like you. Thankfully, God designed parenthood to work even while we are frazzled, feeling as if we have only half a brain. He has placed your child with you and given you all the time you need to parent your child for confidence. This book will equip you to do it well, through the ordinary pace of family life, in the everyday choices of life and through the messiness of relationships.

Second, I want to say that we are all on a journey of developing confidence. You don't need to have got it all sorted. Our goal isn't to say, 'Look at me, kids. I'm super-confident and sorted. Be like me!' Our goal is to position our hearts so that we say, 'God has a great life planned for us and has given us a way to be confident every day, everywhere. I want that for myself and I want it for you, so let's go on the journey together of discovering God's best way for us.'

Third, this book is not just for parents. It's for anyone and everyone who is in a place of influence with children. If you are a foster carer, grandparent, godparent, older sibling, uncle or aunt, children's leader, senior pastor, teacher or anyone else who has input into children's lives, then this book is for you. Please don't feel excluded because I primarily use the term 'parents'.

Fourth, this book is the third in a trilogy of parenting books. If you are at the beginning of spiritually parenting your children and you want some answers on how to start getting them not just to know about God but to be truly connected with God, heart to heart, then you might want to read my book *Parenting Children for a Life of Faith* (BRF, 2010). It's about how we can position ourselves as parents to help our children walk in a vibrant relationship with God, and it will help you coach your children to have a close, personal, two-way relationship with God through prayer. It contains tools to help you connect your children to God's voice and to help them when they feel far from him. In addition, if you want your children to know that they have a powerful purpose on this earth, and you want to coach them in how to walk with God, feeling that every day matters, you might want to read *Parenting Children for a Life of Purpose* (BRF, 2014). It will help you empower your children for their purpose today, and will prepare them for what God is asking them to do in the future.

Fifth, given that you are a busy parent, I wanted to make this book as accessible as it can be for you. I have arranged the book into three sections so that you can navigate through it with ease and can find information quickly.

- The first section, 'Foundations', explores the biblical foundations of our core of confidence. For some of us, this will be a new way of thinking. A biblical understanding of the core of confidence will help us as we go forward, parenting from a viewpoint based on God's word.
- The second section, 'Key tools', describes the approaches we can use to help us parent our children for confidence. I shall refer to these tools throughout the rest of the book.

- The third section, 'Everyday applications', looks at different specific parenting moments, and explores how these moments can be used to enable us to build confidence in our children.

All the stories I use in this book are true and come from people I am working with or have worked with in the past. You will soon add your own stories to the mix. Join me as we explore together how to raise our children to face the broken world clear-eyed and full of confidence, joyfully living in the freedom that Jesus has purchased for them.

May God fill you with peace and hope as you read these pages. May he speak to you and guide your thoughts with clarity. May he give you fantastic sleep and wonderful, precious times with him. And most of all, may you see the fruit of your heart and your parenting as your children grow in their personal confidence in God and in their love for him.

*

Section 1

Foundations

*

— Chapter 2 —

It's not about me

For you have been my hope, Sovereign Lord, my confidence since my youth.

PSALM 71:5

> **God is awesome and holy** and he loves me totally and unreasonably.

We are not the first ones to go on this journey of confidence. We may think that self-esteem is a fairly modern preoccupation, but self-centredness is timeless. Over and over again in scripture, we find people confronting situations with the same questions that we have. In today's culture, we may read these stories with our own filters, so it is helpful to go back and look at solid examples, from different times and circumstances, of how God shaped those people like us who asked the very same questions.

Moses

One of my favourite people in the Bible is Moses. I will mention him a lot in this book, as he must have had a lot of confidence. He was raised in a palace as a member of the Egyptian royal family, ran away and spent years as a shepherd in the desert, and then God gave him the biggest and most nerve-racking job ever. His job was (1) to say incredibly unpopular things to the king of his empire, whom he had known since he was a child; (2) to demand, in essence, the economic collapse of his childhood nation by calling for its slaves to be released; (3) to speak God's words consistently while the country he had lived in for half his life was being devastated by plagues; and (4) to lead a huge number of people into a desert and deal with their whining, complaining and rebellion for the next 40 years. This was not an easy gig, and definitely not in Moses' skill set.

Take a look at how it begins. God calls to Moses from a burning bush and tells him that he is God, and Moses responds with deep reverence. God then pours out his purpose and calls Moses to take part in it.

The Lord said, 'I have seen the troubles my people have suffered in Egypt, and I have heard their cries when the Egyptian slave masters hurt them. I am concerned about their pain, and I have come down to save them from the Egyptians. I will bring them out of that land and lead them to a good land with lots of room—a fertile land. It is the land of the Canaanites, Hittites, Amorites, Perizzites, Hivites, and Jebusites. I have heard the cries of the people of Israel, and I have seen the way the Egyptians have made life hard for them. So now I am sending you to the king of Egypt. Go! Bring my people, the Israelites, out of Egypt!' (Exodus 3:7–10, NCV)

God himself talks to Moses through the miracle of a constantly burning bush and reveals his plan to rescue the Israelites supernaturally, but where is Moses' focus? How does he instantly respond? Does he say, 'Oh, God, you are powerful and mighty. Thank you for hearing your people's cry. Thank you for preparing a land of wonder and provision. You are faithful and I trust you'? No. Moses' first response to hearing this amazing news is to take a good hard look at himself and reply with a question that we will all understand: 'I am not a great man! How can I go to the king and lead the Israelites out of Egypt?' (3:11, NCV).

This is not a surprising question for Moses to ask. Numbers 12:3 tells us that he was 'a very humble man, more humble than anyone else on the face of the earth'. God loves humility. Moses' humility was one of the reasons why God chose him. When faced with such a monumental task, Moses saw his own smallness and asked the question, 'Who am I to do this?'

From our perspective, we might expect God to respond, 'Moses, you know royal court etiquette. You know about shepherding, which is just like leading people. You know the desert. You have all the experiences and skills you need to do this job well. You're not such a crazy choice. Be confident in who you are. You will be great!' But that isn't where God wants Moses to focus. I absolutely love God's response. He simply ignores Moses' question and gives him the only answer he really needs: 'I will be with you' (3:12).

I believe that God's answer to us when we ask 'Who am I?' is the same as the one he gave to Moses. He tells us who *he* is and where *he* will be, because that's the only permanent truth in which we can have confidence.

God goes on, in Exodus 3:14—4:9, to tell Moses how to answer the people's questions, giving him clear instructions, along with displays of his own power and might.

Then something very familiar happens. For me, this is one of those passages of scripture that play in my mind and make me fully aware of my weaknesses and the dangers that lie within them. After God has revealed so much of himself—his heart, his power, his plans and his will—Moses brings the conversation back to himself. You see, he still doesn't feel confident enough. He's still not ready to say, 'It's not about me. It's about you.'

But Moses said to the Lord, 'Please, Lord, I have never been a skilled speaker. Even now, after talking to you, I cannot speak well. I speak slowly and can't find the best words.' Then the Lord said to him, 'Who made a person's mouth? And who makes someone deaf or not able to speak? Or who gives a person sight or blindness? It is I, the Lord. Now go! I will help you speak, and I will teach you what to say.' (Exodus 4:10–12, NCV)

Moses looks at himself and decides that the God of the universe's plan to use him is a terrible idea, because his own view of himself is in the way. Again, though, God does not respond to shore up Moses' belief in himself; God highlights his own absolute ability to make up for any and all weaknesses that Moses may have. For many of us, that would be the end of the discussion, but Moses is a stubborn man. Even after God's assurance that he himself made all mouths, that he shapes the ability to speak or not to speak, to see or not to see, and that he will teach Moses all he needs to know, Moses still can't do it. He says, 'Please, Lord, send someone else' (4:13, NCV).

Moses' inability to put God's ability and character at

the centre of his confidence causes him to reject outright the opportunity that God has for him. Just think about that. How many opportunities has God placed before us, which we didn't take because our view of ourselves was more important than our trust and belief in God? I never, ever want my child to turn down God when he calls because my child thinks he is not suitable for the task. The answer isn't to bolster my son's view of himself so that he says, 'Yes, I am worthy to be used.' The answer is to shape his confidence so that when God says, 'I will do this and I want you to do it with me,' my son will say, 'That seems totally impossible, God, but I'm excited to be a part of what you are doing. I trust that you will teach me what I need to know and that you will pour your grace on everything I think I'm unable to do.' When Moses rejects God's choice and says, 'Please, Lord, send somebody else,' he is essentially saying, 'I don't trust you to work in me,' and God responds with deep emotion:

The Lord became angry with Moses and said, 'Your brother Aaron, from the family of Levi, is a skilled speaker. He is already coming to meet you, and he will be happy when he sees you. You will speak to Aaron and tell him what to say. I will help both of you to speak and will teach you what to do. Aaron will speak to the people for you. You will tell him what God says, and he will speak for you. Take your walking stick with you, and use it to do the miracles.' (Exodus 4:14–17, NCV)

God is faithful to his choice of Moses because he is a faithful God, so he works with Moses and his fears by sending Moses' brother to help him. A small part of me, though, always wonders what it would have looked like had Moses said from the start, 'It's not about me. It's about you, Lord.'

Jesus

We can see this God-centred focus most clearly in Jesus' ministry. Jesus talks to a Samaritan woman at a well, on his way home from a ministry trip (John 4:1–42), and he recognises that she has great needs. She has had a series of five husbands and she is willing to be in a relationship with a man who is not her husband, in a time and place where that arrangement wasn't acceptable. Having a series of husbands could create insecurity in anybody, as it apparently had done in her. Many scholars point to the fact that she came alone to the well at noon, instead of coming during the cool of the morning or evening when the rest of the women of the community would have been there. This subtle detail indicates how lonely and isolated she probably was.[1]

Jesus sees the Samaritan woman's need and responds. Nowadays, many of us would leap into this situation with words of encouragement to bolster her confidence: 'You are worth so much more than this. You deserve a happy life in a committed relationship. You are beautiful and clever and funny, and you are just as good as the other women around. God thinks you are amazing.' Jesus doesn't do this, though. He doesn't flatter her. He doesn't try to convince her of her good qualities or tell her how perfect she is, just the way God made her. He doesn't respond to her insecurity by trying to shore up her self-image. His response to her need is simple.

He tells her about himself. He tells her that he is the Messiah and that he can give her 'a spring of water welling up to eternal life' (v. 14). His response to her life situation is to show her more of God, not more of herself.

Throughout scripture

Over and over again in scripture we see God talking with people in this way. Gideon was a farmer whom God commanded to lead an army to save Israel. When Gideon asked, 'Lord, how can I save Israel? My family group is the weakest in Manasseh, and I am the least important member of my family,' God answered, 'I will be with you. It will seem as if the Midianites you are fighting are only one man' (Judges 6:15–16, NCV). To take another example, Job was a wealthy man whose world collapsed. When he questioned God about it, God responded by highlighting the breadth of his almighty power and glory: 'Where were you when I laid the earth's foundations?' (Job 38:4).

God makes it very clear that our confidence should not be in ourselves or our capabilities. Confidence is not a denying of ourselves; it is a recentring of what is important. When we place ourselves aside and put God in the centre, then something wonderful happens: we get to dream bigger. Moses adjusted his core of confidence and saw the end of 400 years of slavery in Egypt and the establishment of a nation. Mary was a teenager going about her daily life when the angel appeared to her and told her she would give birth to the Saviour of the world. She responded not with the question

'Why me?' but with a heart of amazement and gratitude toward God. Mary, then, had the joy of raising Jesus, the Son of God. The Samaritan woman placed her confidence in God and had her hope renewed. As a result, her entire town responded to her words and ran out to meet Jesus.

While Jesus was praying in Gethsemane, he told God the Father, 'Not my will, but yours be done' (Luke 22:42). Jesus' confidence in his Father's will was such that he was able to endure the unimaginable horrors of the cross and redeem us and all humanity.

Paul faced down venomous snakes, shipwrecks, a stoning, kings and imprisonment because he knew, 'We worship God through his Spirit, and our pride is in Christ Jesus. We do not put trust in ourselves or anything we can do' (Philippians 3:3, NCV). By keeping his confidence in God, Paul was able to play a part in spreading the gospel across the entire Roman empire.

Again and again in scripture we see that those who put their confidence in who God is, and not in who they are, are the ones who carry the peace, love, joy, and power of God with them. When we focus on ourselves, our frailty and imperfections become huge, and our view shrinks so that we see only our weaknesses. But when we truly believe that God is awesomely wonderful, and we put our confidence in him, then we can live freely. We can catch God's heart for the world, and we can believe that we might be a small part of his grand plans. When our children take on this belief, they will look at school and see God's heart for their friends and communities. They will see injustice and want to do something about it. They will see pain and want to respond.

They will no longer limit their dreams and hopes to what they feel they are capable of doing, but they will broaden their dreams to what God is able to do and will recognise when he wants to do it.

> God is awesome and holy, **and he loves me totally and unreasonably.**

I am loved

When Moses asked who God was, and God revealed himself, God said two things, not one:

God said to Moses, 'I am who I am. This is what you are to say to the Israelites: "I am has sent me to you."' God also said to Moses, 'Say to the Israelites, "The Lord, the God of your fathers—the God of Abraham, the God of Isaac and the God of Jacob—has sent me to you." This is my name forever, the name you shall call me from generation to generation.' (Exodus 3:14–15)

We always focus on the big, booming 'I am who I am' part of this passage, but I find it interesting that 'I am who I am' isn't the complete picture. In the other half of the statement, God declares his ongoing relationship with people. He says, essentially, 'I am God, and for a very long time I have been in relationship with you and your family.' Relationship is very much a part of God, and we need to train our children to see God through the lens of relationship, through the lens of his love.

The apostle Paul's prayer was 'that you... may have power, together with all the Lord's holy people, to grasp how wide and long and high and deep is the love of Christ' (Ephesians 3:17–18). God's love is complete and unconditional. We cannot earn it, lose it or deserve it, and we definitely aren't worthy of it. We are loved because he chooses to love us. He made us, and his love for us is the foundation of our confidence.

Throughout scripture, we are assured of God's deep love for us. It is undeserved and unreasonable; he simply loves us. In order for the impact of his love to hit home for our children, two things need to happen: they need to understand his love in context, and they need to be trained to see and feel God's love.

Who loves me?

Our children are loved by many people, including parents, grandparents, aunts, uncles, siblings and friends. Some people can communicate deep love well, while others mention love only casually in cards for birthdays or Christmas. Children care about who loves them, and the more important a person is to their lives, the more that person's love matters.

If a stranger walks up to you and declares her permanent friendship for you, you won't instantly celebrate and invite her round to your house for cake and tea. No matter how much she insists on her feelings of friendship for you, the encounter will feel weird because you are strangers. But if you and she spend lots of time together, and you discover that she is kind and funny and generous and humble, something might begin to shift in your thinking. Your respect for her will grow. You will admire her, celebrate her and find her amazing and delightful. Then, when she turns to you and says, 'I so love being your friend, just as you are right now. I cherish our friendship. There is nothing you could do to make me love you more as my friend, and there is nothing you can do that would ever change my feelings,' you will feel deeply loved.

The first key concept in the core of confidence is crucial for children to understand: God is awesome and holy, *and* he loves me totally and unreasonably.

When we talk with children, we often talk about God's love, separate from who he is, focusing more on love than on the one doing the loving. The more children get to know God and how wonderful he is, the more they can be lifted up by the knowledge of his faithful and gigantic love for them.

How do I know?

In order to help our children access God's love, we need to teach them how to see God's love, how to understand God's love, and how to encounter God's love personally, so that their connection with him will last a lifetime.

One summer I met a ten-year-old boy at an event I was running. He had a stutter and was desperately shy. All of us workers had spent a whole week with the children, exploring the character of God—who he is, and how awesome and holy he is. The boy told me that he was tired of being scared all the time and that he wanted to talk with God about it. I sat down next to him, placed my hand on his shoulder and asked God to meet with him, speak to him and give him everything he needed. As we sat side by side in silence, the boy engaged with God in his mind and heart, chatting back and forth. Eventually, a smile slowly spread across his face. We were both quiet for about five minutes while he sat with his eyes closed, quietly smiling and praying. At one point he gently raised his hand and put it on his own chest.

After a while, I asked him what God was doing. He opened his eyes and glowed as he told me that God had put his hand on his chest 'right here', patting his hand over his heart. 'God told me he has spent every day with me, and that I make him laugh with happiness, and that he is my real dad. My biological father left when I was tiny, and my mum is a single mum, but God wants to be my dad! I can still feel his hand!' Not once did the boy stutter while he told me about his encounter with God, and I had the privilege of watching him walk tall and laugh loudly and look freer than I had ever seen him before.

When we train our children to know powerfully that 'God is awesome and holy and he loves me totally and unreasonably', it roots them in a relationship with God that lasts a lifetime. I think that when Jesus said he had come to give us life, and life to the full (John 10:10), this was part of what he meant. Confidence comes from knowing and experiencing the fact that it isn't about us; it's about him. In his glory and wonder, he turns his heart and his face towards us and loves us completely and totally.

*

Chapter 3

I'm not finished yet

Blessed is the one who trusts in the Lord, whose
confidence is in him. They will be like a tree planted
by the water that sends out its roots by the stream. It
does not fear when heat comes; its leaves are always
green. It has no worries in a year of drought and
never fails to bear fruit.

JEREMIAH 17:7–8

God is awesome and holy, and he loves me
totally and unreasonably.

**He is daily shaping me to be like him, and I
am not finished yet.**

I am invited to be a small part of his wonderful
plans.

Perfection

We live in a world where perfection is king. We describe
our ultimate ideal as 'perfect', whether it be a person we
love, an experience on holiday, or the way a meal is cooked.
Perfection is something to be prized and achieved, and we
expect it to be the goal of leaders, colleagues and spouses

alike. Many people seek to appear 'perfect' to others, in terms of their happiness, job satisfaction, achievements and family life. We can sometimes hide our flaws so people will think we are closer to the ideal than we actually are. Everyday life is warped on television and in movies, presenting a more 'perfect' reality than the one around us. We can spend a lot of spiritual and emotional energy in trying to appear as personally perfect as possible and working to perfection in our home life and work. Unfortunately, our children are not spared from the scrutiny.

This value of 'perfection' is damaging our children. They feel their imperfections and they begin to look at themselves through new eyes as they learn that anything less than perfection is failure. Consequently, we try to make them feel better by assuring them of their perfection. We insist that they are perfect 'just the way they are'. We assure them that God sees them as perfect. We try to redefine 'perfection' for them so that it is achievable today. Perfection isn't seen as a journey; it's seen as an expectation for *now*, and one in which our children will constantly fail.

Objectively, we know that perfection is not attainable. None of us is without flaws; none of us has achieved perfection. So why do we allow our children to think that perfection is the ultimate goal and that they have achieved it 'just by being them'?

The truth is much more liberating. Paul tells us, 'All have sinned and fall short of the glory of God' (Romans 3:23). Jesus lived on earth and died and rose again in order to pay the price for our imperfection and provide the grace and mercy required to give us a close relationship with God and freedom from sin. It is impossible for us to generate our own perfection, which is why God became perfection for us.

The truth is that each of us, child and adult alike, is on a journey with God, a journey of transformation to become more and more like our Father. We are on a lifelong journey of being shaped by God to reflect his glory and to be effective and purposeful wherever he plants us. What that truth means for us is that, at any one point in our lives, we are only partially through our journey of transformation.

I see it like this. Picture a baker who is creating a beautiful wedding cake. The design is already complete and the cake has been paid for. All the components for a masterpiece are in place. The baker then takes the ingredients and begins to shape the mix into a batter. How foolish we would be if we popped our heads into the bakery and scoffed at the bowl of cake mix, dismissing it because it didn't look like a wedding cake! It will be a cake one day, but this is only the first step. The baker has plans for the mix: he wants it to go through more processing and finessing. It will undergo many stages before it is unveiled as the perfect wedding cake, but the baker already sees what the finished product will look like.

We would be foolish, too, to look in on the baker with his mixing bowl in hand and announce that the cake he's stirring is absolutely complete and perfect just as it is, and that no more work needs to be done. We can't celebrate it as a finished cake, because it isn't finished yet. However, we can sample the mix and cherish the stage that it's in, appreciating it for the potential it holds. We can appreciate the hints of the final design in its current state, and we can help in the kitchen, acting as partners with the baker in his work.

Unlike a cake mix, though, our children can be active partners with God in their own growth. Our delight as parents is to empower our children to embrace the stage they are in, instead of judging themselves for not being complete. We can train our children to be in proactive partnership with God and us as they embrace their current stage of transformation and boldly move toward the next.

Personality versus character

We can often forget that there is a difference between personality and character. For the purposes of this discussion, I mean that personality, broadly, is the set of predispositions we were born with, the way we are genetically wired to encounter the world. It includes our openness to new experiences and ideas, our drive for stimulation, how comfortable we are with others, and our responses to negative emotions such as stress and anxiety.[2] Some psychologists assert that babies come into the world with these things hardwired into them and, even before their births, we can begin to notice the differences in their personalities. Personality rarely, if ever, changes.

Character, on the other hand, is constantly growing and changing. It is the way we apply our personalities, faith, values and beliefs and engage with the world. It governs our choices and, eventually, our behaviour. Character is about sacrifice and perseverance, integrity and forgiveness, generosity in the face of need, choosing joy in adversity, and more.

We are called as parents to celebrate our children's personalities and disciple their characters. A child's personality may mean that he naturally dislikes new experiences, for example, but the way we encourage that child to wrestle with his fear and develop an appreciation for bravely adventuring into the unknown is all part of parenting his character.

God's journey with us

This is what God does with us. God seeks to draw us into relationship with him through the freedom he provided for us on the cross, and he desires to take us on a lifelong journey of transformation to be more like him.

The Lord is the Spirit, and where the Spirit of the Lord is, there is freedom. Our faces, then, are not covered. We all show the Lord's glory, and we are being changed to be like him. This change in us brings ever greater glory, which comes from the Lord, who is the Spirit. (2 Corinthians 3:17–18, NCV)

Throughout our lives, we know that we are not complete yet: we are on a journey of transformation. When we embrace that knowledge, it will bring freedom and joy into our lives. We won't expect ourselves to be perfect, because we'll recognise that it is an impossible goal. All we can do is humble our hearts to be content in all things, and engage fully with God as he transforms our hearts and minds. God is faithful to take us on a glorious journey, and we can trust in his faithfulness to take our children on a glorious journey, too.

Paul once wrote that he was 'confident of this, that he who began a good work in you will carry it on to completion until the day of Christ Jesus' (Philippians 1:6). God loves our children; he is faithful each day to lead them gently and wisely on a journey of transformation, and we are partners with him and our children in that lifelong process. What would our children's lives be like if they were perfectly content to be who they are in all their imperfections? What would their lives be like if they were perfectly content to be where they are on their journey, with hope and joyful anticipation for the future?

We don't have to be perfect to be useful

God is awesome and holy, and he loves me totally and unreasonably.

He is daily shaping me to be like him, and I am not finished yet.

I am invited to be a small part of his wonderful plans.

The wonderful thing about God is that he doesn't wait for us to be complete or perfect before using us in powerful and purposeful ways in this world. God is already in the world rescuing people, awakening their hearts and ministering to their minds, and, no matter where we are on our journey of transformation, he invites us to act as partners with him.

To be partners with God is an undeserved honour, as well as a key part of our own transformation process. While we are on our muddled journeys of transformation, we get to see God work. We can be a small part of his wonderful plans on this earth, all because of his grace and faithfulness. Whether we are mature in Christ or brand new to God, whether we are old or young, our relationship with God invites us into purpose.

Our weakness and incompleteness create space for God's power. The default setting in our heads screams that confidence comes from within, from feeling calm and secure in ourselves. When we believe this, though, we miss out on one of the great truths of God: it is precisely in our weakness, our brokenness and our inability that God moves in power.

Paul was a man who hated Jesus' followers and persecuted them fiercely until Jesus appeared to him on the road to Damascus and turned his life upside down. Paul then began a long journey of personal transformation, slowly becoming one of our greatest heroes of faith. It took time. In one of his letters to the church in Corinth, Paul described himself as a weak jar of clay that held the treasure of God's light, God's truth: 'But we have this treasure in jars of clay to show that this all-surpassing power is from God and not from us' (2 Corinthians 4:7).

For Paul, his human weakness and incompleteness enabled him to live with the obvious power of God in his life. Once, Paul wrote that he had pleaded with God three times to solve a personal problem.

But [God] said to me, 'My grace is sufficient for you, for my power is made perfect in weakness.' Therefore I will boast all the more gladly about my weaknesses, so that Christ's power may rest on me. That is why, for Christ's sake, I delight in weaknesses, in insults, in hardships, in persecutions, in difficulties. For when I am weak, then I am strong. (2 Corinthians 12:9–10)

For our children

Our children are not perfect, nor should they be. Because God loves them, he is daily transforming them to be more like him. Our children will learn that throughout their journeys, God's power will be strong, even in their weaknesses. He invites them to do wonderful things with him, to be a small part of his great plans for this earth.

When our children know deep down the freedom that comes from being on this journey with a God who pours his grace around their weaknesses, then an unshakeable confidence will begin to grow within them.

*

Section 2

Key tools

*

— Chapter 4 —

Introduction of hearts and minds

Confidence is a tricky thing, and it can seem an intangible and slippery idea for children. How do we approach the task of building a deep and positive core of confidence within our children? What tools can we use?

Throughout scripture God seems very concerned with our hearts and our minds, because he often refers to them. Sometimes he just talks about our hearts and sometimes he just talks about our minds, but often he talks about the two together. For example, God tells Jeremiah, 'I the Lord search the heart and examine the mind' (Jeremiah 17:10). Then, when a Pharisee questions Jesus about the greatest commandment, Jesus answers by quoting an Old Testament verse: 'Love the Lord your God with all your heart and with all your soul and with all your mind' (Matthew 22:37; compare Deuteronomy 6:5).

The apostle Paul writes that people's 'thinking became futile and their foolish hearts were darkened' (Romans 1:21). In his letter to the Philippians, Paul encourages believers by writing that when they pray, 'the peace of God, which transcends all understanding, will guard your hearts and your minds in Christ Jesus' (Philippians 4:7).

As we begin to train our children in confidence, we can use the idea of 'the heart and the mind' as a useful focus, because the heart and the mind are often our battlegrounds in the fight for confidence in our children.

What do we mean by 'heart' and 'mind'? Each one of us might describe these concepts differently, but, for the purposes of this book, I have defined them broadly as follows. The heart involves:

- Feelings
- Spiritual concepts (for example, purity, sin)
- Pain and suffering
- Instincts, reactions, responses born of experience
- Relationships
- Personality

The mind involves:

- Thinking
- Perception
- Decisions and choices
- Attention
- Wonderings and ponderings
- Judgements
- Character

True confidence is rooted in both the heart and the mind. For example, we want our children to feel deeply confident (the heart) and we want them to choose confidently (the mind). We also want them not to be afraid, but to be able to respond freely and confidently to people and situations (the heart), while we also desire them to look at themselves and other people with humble confidence and clarity (the mind).

These are by no means perfect definitions. You may not even feel that they are good ones, so feel free to disagree and swap things around. In essence, I want us to understand that God is concerned with both the heart and the mind, and we as parents are called to give our attention to both of them in our children. Different tools are needed to nurture and develop our children's hearts and to train and shape their minds. Here in Section 2 we will look at the tools we can use to draw close to our children's hearts and minds, in order to build a life of confidence in them.

— Chapter 5 —

Hearts

> For this people's heart has become calloused; they
> hardly hear with their ears, and they have closed
> their eyes. Otherwise they might see with their eyes,
> hear with their ears, understand with their hearts
> and turn, and I would heal them.
>
> MATTHEW 13:15

> Blessed are the pure in heart, for they will see God.
>
> MATTHEW 5:8

My husband and I once owned two tiny yucca trees, George
and Malachi (yes, we name our plants). We bought them for
our wedding with the oh-so-grand and romantic intention
of growing them through our entire lives and then having
them planted on our graves when we died. After about three
months they began to look... wrong. Not wilted. Not dead.
Just... off. The trunks were a bit too squidgy and the leaves
were a bit too sticky. The colour was inconsistent. Nothing
was catastrophic, things were just wrong. After six months
we knew something bad was happening, but we couldn't
figure it out. We had followed all the advice on the little card.
We couldn't make sense of it.

One day George and Malachi just fell over. Then we
discovered that their roots had completely rotted. The main
source of their health, of their life, had rotted away, and we
hadn't even noticed.

What happens to a plant's roots is crucial to its overall health and well-being. Those roots may be buried deep underground and may spread so far and wide that it is impossible to know all the areas from which the plant draws its nutrients. We notice something is wrong with the root system only when the effects finally begin to show up on the plant.

I feel that something similar often happens to our children, particularly in terms of their hearts. We see the effect of hidden influences in their lives, whether it is fear, shame, anger, hesitance, unreasonable desire or stubborn refusal. Sometimes we instinctively sense that there is something underneath their behaviour, something happening in their hearts, but we feel ill-equipped to find out what it is. This perception arises especially in areas of confidence because confidence touches upon such deep feelings and experiences in our children.

There are key tools that we can use to access our children's hearts, so that we can monitor the health of their roots. Root issues can only be sorted at the root level. For something like confidence, we need to have a good handle on how to nurture our children's hearts at the root level.

Exploring together

Our children often can't understand what they are feeling, much less why they are feeling it. In the course of everyday life, our job is to help them negotiate that emotional path, and, if we are particularly intent on developing our children's confidence, it is even more important that we do so.

When we can understand what they are feeling, when we can truly get alongside their hearts and see what is happening underneath their behaviour, then we can help them grow healthy roots, emotionally and spiritually. Time constraints can trap us into disciplining outward behaviour instead of discipling hearts, but confidence is nearly impossible to correct from the outside. We need to get into their hearts.

No matter how much pruning, music playing and encouraging talk you give a plant, if the roots are damaged or are drawing from a poisoned source, then the plant will suffer. If we never learn to address our children's hearts, we miss our opportunity to be as effective as we might be.

Four tools for drawing close to children's hearts

Understand through curiosity

Children can smell an agenda a mile away. In your relationship with your children, develop a regular pattern of asking them questions just to understand them better. This can be a helpful tool in getting snapshots of your children's hearts without any of you feeling the pressure to do something. So often we look at our children's hearts with a clumsy surgeon's approach: we want to fix the damage quickly, so we ask questions with an obvious agenda to fix something right then and there. As a result, some of our children shut down emotionally before we can make any progress. However, if we begin having conversations just to develop a culture of understanding, like taking a temperature or testing the level of chemicals in water, our children will feel more comfortable with the questions and much less threatened by the process.

As parents, we may stop long enough to understand the problem but not take time to drill down into how our child actually sees the problem. This approach goes beyond just having good listening skills. It's about working in partnership with God and your child to understand your child's heart, not just to understand the presented problem. It means keeping the conversation going until you can accurately say, 'Ah, I see. To you it looks like this and feels like this. I understand!' and your child can say in return, 'Yes. That's it!' This kind of interaction stirs your compassion: you understand not just what the child's mind is thinking, but also how her heart feels, which is what we are aiming to shape. Our first achievement is not to fix the problem, but to understand it.

Good conversations often start with something that makes you ponder. It may be the huge fight you had with your child or a tiny inflection in your child's voice. God will poke you as you notice a hesitation in a sentence or a reaction that doesn't seem quite right—a little thing, revealing that there may be a part of your child's roots that is not in the best condition.

Be genuinely curious and willing to go down the rabbit hole for the pure sake of understanding. We all long to be understood. When we genuinely set our hearts to want to understand our child and to see through his eyes, then we are on the path to building true heart connections with our child. It doesn't take much more time than a regular conversation. It just means continuing a little to see how far it goes. Most of these conversations take five minutes, and they can be done while in the car, walking to school, cuddling in bed or making dinner. Just set your heart to be curious, and start asking. As your child is talking, ask open-ended questions or make statements that follow what your child is saying, with no real direction or end goal. Here are a few examples:

- Tell me more about [xxx]. That sounds interesting!
- What would happen if…?
- Does it feel more like this, or like this?
- Why? Why not?
- What are you afraid might happen?
- How did that make you feel?
- You seem to be feeling [xxx]. Is that true?
- What happened to make you feel that way? When did it start?
- We can decide that later. Now I just want to understand better. So tell me more about [xxx].

When you think you understand—when you think you can see the situation from the child's eyes—summarise it for them in the way that you think they would put it. 'I see. This is what you think and feel? This is how it looks to you? Wow!' Affirm their emotions while they're at the bottom of the hole. Once you understand and can say, 'I see!' then it's important that you meet them with empathy and compassion, no matter how crazy the problem looks to you. Of course they are feeling what they are feeling. Look at how they see it.

When my son had just turned four, he went through a time of hiding his wounds. He would instantly show his little cuts or bruises to whichever parent was around, and we would comfort him and treat them. After the initial treatment, though, we noticed that he would try to hide the wound. He would cry if we wanted to look at it, and he would become deeply embarrassed and uncomfortable. If he got knocked at the swimming pool, he would be incredibly self-conscious and not want anyone to look at his bumps.

We, of course, began to be concerned about this. It was affecting his confidence with friends and other adults. We knew his wounds weren't caused by anything very serious because we were with him when he got them. We thought maybe he was afraid of being judged or mocked. When we asked him about it, he said he didn't want people to feel bad. We assumed that meant he didn't want people to comment or ask about it. We thought he was embarrassed, and we became very concerned about what this meant for his future in terms of his body image.

One day I decided to find out more. I wanted to ask questions until I could really and truly see the issue from his view, without judging or worrying. I just wanted to understand. The next time it happened, I asked him why he didn't want me to see the tiny scratch on his knee.

'I don't want you to feel bad,' he replied.

'Why would I feel bad?' I asked.

'You would say, "Oooo, that looks like it would hurt!" and then it would hurt you.' He placed his hand over the tiny scratch.

I was confused. 'It would hurt me because I say "Ooooooo" as if it hurts me?'

'Yes!' he said, and then he started crying.

I moved in closer. 'Oh, babe, it doesn't hurt my body when I see your owies. Is that why you hide them?'

'Yes... no. I don't want you to be hurt.' He struggled to explain himself.

'Tell me more. What else are you worried about?'

'I'm afraid you'll be... disappointed!' And with that he started sobbing.

Now I have never, ever used the word 'disappointed' in our relationship, but for some reason he was worried about it. I rubbed his hand gently. 'Oh, honey, you are worried about disappointing me? What are you afraid of? What do you think would happen if I were disappointed?'

The sobs continued in earnest. 'I'm scared you will throw me away!'

'Oh, my son! That sounds very scary!'

'Yesssss.' The wails went on.

Respond with empathy and bring truth

Once we get to the bottom of the issue, it is important that we respond with empathy and understanding. Too many times, after we have uncovered something in our children's hearts, we respond with our emotions: we laugh at the silliness of the fear; we become angry that they have never told us their fear before; we are shocked at their behaviour or thoughts, or we are visibly relieved. When we allow that to happen, we can lose the influence of the moment because our children then respond to our emotion instead of staying focused on their issue and on what we want to say. I would encourage you to find that place of compassion and understanding within yourself from which you can respond to your children's hearts in the moment with genuine concern, peace and love.

The next question to consider is this: what is the truth that needs to be spoken here?

At this vulnerable moment in the conversation, we often try to bring in our oh-so-wise judgement, either positive or negative. What is needed, though, is not our judgement; what is needed is the truth. Our children don't need us to say, 'Don't think that!' or 'What a silly thing to feel!' What they feel is what they feel, and that's OK. In this moment we need to ask ourselves and God what truth would restore health to our child's roots, and then decide if now is the moment when that truth can be sown.

'Oh, my son, look into my eyes,' I said. I lifted up his chin and then I began to place truth into his heart. 'I will never, ever, ever throw you away. I love you. There is nothing you can do that will make me stop loving you. There is no part of your body, inside or out, that can be broken bad enough to make me want to throw you away. My love is so big for you, as big as my whole body, and Daddy God's love is even stronger because his heart is gi-normous! Do I love you when you are sweet?'

'Yes,' his little voice came back. He gave a smile.

'Do I love you when you yell, when you are angry?'

'No,' he said. His chin started to wobble.

'*Yes!*' I said. 'I love you bigger than the whole world,

even when you are angry. There is nothing that can make me stop loving you.'

His eyes widened.

'Do I love you when you laugh?' I asked.

'Yes.'

'Do I love you when you don't listen to me?'

'No...'

'*Yes!* I love you so much, even when you don't listen to me. There is nothing that can make me stop loving you.'

A smile broke across his face.

'Do I love you when you cuddle with me?'

'Yes!'

'Do I love you when you throw things?'

He paused for a long moment and then he shouted, 'Yes!'

'Yes, I do!' I shouted back in agreement. 'I love you more than Christmas, even when you throw things. There is nothing that can make me stop loving you. I love you when you are sweet. I love you when you are angry. I love you when you laugh and when you don't listen, when we cuddle and when you throw things. There is nothing that can make me or God or Daddy stop loving you or ever want to throw you away. Nothing!'

He jumped up and flung his arms around my neck.

Connect your children to yourself and God

Our heart connection with our children is incredibly important. It's what allows us to wade into the deep parts of their heart, so we need to set aside a time for them to connect with us, even if it's only a brief moment. God is the only one who can truly mend hearts and transform minds, so to give our children the opportunity to meet with him is very important.

As my son hugged me, I whispered, 'Oh, Daddy God, thank you for making Caleb and me family. Thank you that you love us more than we can even think of and that you will never throw us away! My heart is so happy right now, God.'

'Me too, God,' Caleb whispered.

Help children to be powerful for the next time

We want children to remember the truth they have learned and to remember how they dealt with the situation, so that if the problem arises again, they will be able to handle it powerfully. They need a plan, and we can help them make one.

'Hey, wait a minute,' I said to Caleb. 'Daddy has some cuts on his legs. Let's look! Do you want to throw Daddy away because he has those cuts?'

'*Noooo!*' Caleb exclaimed. 'I love Daddy for ever!'

'That's right!' I said. 'How are our hearts? Are they far away from each other or together again?'

'Together.' He smiled and then let out a sigh.

'OK,' I said. 'So what do you do the next time you have a cut on your body?'

'Don't be scared. Just show it.' He popped up and pointed at each of us. 'We don't hide from each other. We love each other.'

'Absolutely,' I said. 'Now, I'm going to make dinner. What are you going to do?'

Each tool on its own is useful and, sometimes, using one of them in isolation is the most powerful thing you can do. In combination, they allow you to delve quickly and easily into the heart issues affecting your children.

- Understand through curiosity.
- Respond with empathy and bring truth.
- Connect children to yourself and God.
- Help children to be powerful for the next time.

It is so easy to get into the groove of dealing with behaviour that we can miss the opportunity to dig down to the roots of our children's actions. As we look to build children who are spiritually and emotionally confident, our ease and skill in calmly ministering to their hearts will grow, and we will have the joy of shaping confidence from its deepest roots.

When we teach our children's hearts, the lessons stick for a long time. Even now, years later, in the midst of other behaviour discussions, my son will glance up at me or look over his shoulder as he heads to his room and call, 'You still love me a lot, though. That doesn't change!' One good conversation can last a lifetime, because heart lessons produce fruit.

*

Chapter 6

Minds

> You will keep in perfect peace those whose minds are
> steadfast, because they trust in you.
> ISAIAH 26:3

'Are you excited about your new school?' Sonia bent down and helped Ben slip his jumper over his shoulders. She wondered if he could adapt to a new home and a new school so quickly.

Ben nodded his head. 'God chose my school! There were no places there so we had to wait and wait. God moved all the people around so I could be at this school.'

'That's wonderful, Ben!' She checked his hair one more time. 'Are you worried about making new friends?'

'No.' Ben grinned. 'God chose my school, so it's perfect for me. I will find my friends and be kind to them and it will be just right. We fit each other, me and my school.'

What are we talking about when we say 'confidence'? For me, confidence is the combined freedom, peace, strength and joy that come from seeing ourselves, others and the world with a godly mindset. When we parent our children for a life of confidence, we are essentially building and focusing the way our children think. The world is as it is: it is broken and wonderful and sad and heavenly and everything in between. How we perceive it and respond to it all depends on how our mind sees it. Our mind defines reality for us. It is the filter for our lives, the operating system for our choices and relationships and for the way we view ourselves and others. It's the essence of how we approach living.

Have you ever met someone who thought radically differently from you? I have. I was once very ill with ME, bedbound and unable to work. One day my husband came home from work with a big smile on his face. He greeted me with a kiss and announced, 'Guess what, honey? We get to live by faith!' I sat up very confused as he went on. 'I had my six-month review, and they feel that I am not cut out for this type of work, so they aren't going to renew the contract. I'm fired! We get to live by faith. Isn't that cool?' He took his shoes off and hummed to himself as he went to the kitchen to grab a drink.

My brain started freaking out as I saw a hundred million horrible things cascading towards us: no electricity, no place to live, no food and no future. My husband, all the while, happily drank his water and smiled confidently.

At that moment, my mind allowed me to see only money problems and hopelessness, but my husband had trained his mind to see something else entirely. My mind defined the situation as a widening chasm of fear and worry, but my husband's mind enabled him to see a situation where the faithful God who works all things together for the good of those who love him was going to do something wonderful. My husband quickly got another job that worked out much better for our family, and I had to recognise that perhaps my mindset wasn't the best.

Scripture talks a lot about the mind. It often mentions the blessing of a mind rightly aligned. For example, 'If people's thinking is controlled by the sinful self, there is death. But if their thinking is controlled by the Spirit, there is life and peace' (Romans 8:6, NCV).

'Life and peace'. Oh, if we could raise children who truly had fullness of life and a steady and deep daily peace. What a goal!

Various biblical authors give us suggestions for how to set our minds, but I believe Paul sums it up well when he writes, 'Do not be shaped by this world; instead be changed within by a new way of thinking. Then you will be able to decide what God wants for you; you will know what is good and pleasing to him and what is perfect' (Romans 12:2, NCV). Many of us, including our children, don't realise what we are missing by living with the world's mindset.

The day I got glasses, my life changed for ever. I was ten years old and I remember sitting in the car wearing my new glasses and being absolutely fascinated by trees. Did you know that it was possible to see the leaves on trees? I didn't, until that day. The trees weren't just big green blobs any more. I could see the leaves on all the trees *at the same time, from the car*! Until that day, nature had not been a big deal to me because it was just large swathes of colour, but all of a sudden I was amazed by everything. I could read signs. I could see nature. I could recognise friends from across the classroom. I could volunteer to answer problems on the chalkboard. I could play sports and react to the ball before it was within two metres of me. I felt like a superhero with amazing vision. My headaches even went away. It was wonderful! My glasses enabled me to walk and read and write and sightsee and play sports and engage with life confidently because they had been finely tuned to enable me to see the world with clarity. My glasses made all the difference.

I believe that we have this same type of perception problem spiritually. The way we see the world is different from the way we were meant to see it. Over the years, our mind builds a perception of the world. Our parents, family, friends, music, magazines, books, schools and the internet all shape us. We walk through life perceiving ourselves and others through this filter and responding from that perspective. The problem is that those perceptions may not be the ones that God designed for us. The world declares that beauty, money and success are important, that self-worth is based on others' approval, and that happiness should be pursued and won. The fruit of the way the world works is fear, worry, insecurity, fragility and striving.

The life God has for us brings restoration, wholeness, purpose, security and true confidence. The mindset God designs shows us that he is awesome and wonderful and that he is everywhere and active. A godly mindset helps us to live in the knowledge that God loves us totally and completely, imperfect as we are, and that he is daily shaping us to be more and more like him. It enables us to see that God's purposes on earth are mighty and that he has called us to be partners with him to bring beauty from ashes and his rightness on earth.

If our children's view of the world and themselves is of that godly mindset, it will affect every area of their lives—how they look in the mirror, how they feel walking down the street, what they think the moment they walk into school, and even how they react when someone shoves them into a wall or calls them a name. It will shape their boldness in compassion and in trying new things. It will be the fuel for the kind of friends or husbands or wives they will be and, eventually, it will affect the way our grandchildren face the world. A godly mindset empowers children to have a confidence that lasts.

How can we begin to build a godly mindset? How can we teach our children to think and to see themselves, others and the world at large from God's perspective?

An optician's approach

Only you can see through your own eyes. An optician can't see the world exactly as you see it. When she is working with you, her job is to diagnose and treat your eyes primarily by using your feedback, your words and your judgements. Her job is to try to understand what you see as well as she can, but she is unable to know it exactly. Her physical examination helps her make a general guess, and then she knows where to start. She asks you to put on a set of glasses that can be adjusted or she asks you to look through a big machine, and a very subjective process begins.

The optician shows you wall charts of letters or numbers, and she begins to put lenses in front of your eyes. 'Is this one better, or this one?' she asks. 'Number one, or number two?' You answer her questions the best you can. Together, through a series of choices, the two of you narrow down the lenses that are right for you, the ones that give you the sharpest eyesight for your life. It's a partnership. The optician's job is to trust you to answer correctly and to understand how you are seeing now, in order to make the necessary adjustments so that you can see better in the future.

If we are going to position our children's minds well, then we need to have an element of the optician in us. It's not just about deciding what to do and doing it. It's about setting ourselves to walk along a life journey with our children, constantly adjusting the way we parent, to help them develop a godly mindset, which will produce the fruit of true confidence, peace and the knowledge of God's will for them and others.

Five tools for shaping children's minds

Direct attention and values

One way of shaping the way our children perceive and think is by looking at what we draw their attention to and what we give our attention to. Most of the ways we operate in everyday life are almost unconscious. Years of habit have drawn us into behaving and speaking in a certain manner, and our children pick up on our speech and behaviour. It's the little things that shape their perceptions.

For instance, when your child walks into the room, what do you look at first and what do you say? I have a friend whose mum would almost immediately look her up and down and comment on her appearance. Often it was a positive comment, but it created a way of thinking within my friend. She grew up considering personal appearance to be a central part of the way she viewed herself and others, and, therefore, her confidence became rooted in appearances.

When you are out and about with your children, what do you point out to them? Where do you draw their attention? What do you comment on? What do you talk about? What values do you think you are communicating to your children through the topics of conversation that pop up along the road and at home, through what you laugh at and what you roll your eyes at?

Use foundational phrases

Language is one of the key tools for how we think. What we say lays down a framework for understanding. Throughout our children's lives, we will be establishing this skeleton of thinking, this framework, from which all other understanding will hang. Foundational truths lie at the base of everything we do. Every family tends to have favourite phrases or sayings. Some of these are clichés, and some are not. If you think back to your childhood, you may remember some of them: 'if you can't say anything nice, don't say anything at all'; 'hug a tree if you get lost'; 'life's not fair'; 'blessed to be a blessing'. In the movie *Meet the Robinsons*, the characters often repeat, 'Keep moving forward' and 'See a need. Fill a need.' All of these phrases and sayings give children easy-access language for developing helpful values.

But there are also deeper things that parents say, which stick with children—key phrases and ways of responding that embed themselves into our children's brains. I'm sure you have had the experience of hearing your own parents' words accidentally leaping out of your mouth when you're talking to your children. Some phrases just stick in our minds. We as parents have an opportunity to deliberately craft foundational messages that will become part of a framework for our children's thinking.

Verbally frame what children are seeing

Children's brains are constantly trying to make sense of the world—trying to understand, for instance, cause and effect, power in relationships, how culture works and where God is in all of it. One of the most powerful tools you can use is the ability to 'frame' the world for your children. In essence, we help our children to see the world around them, and then we provide understanding so that they can make sense of what they are seeing. We teach them what they are looking at. When our children are under five years old, we do this almost all the time because at this stage of life they are constantly asking 'why?' They draw us into framing the world for them. They ask 'why?' about people and relationships and nature and machines. Unfortunately, as they get older, they often stop asking 'why?' and we forget that the need for framing is still there.

Our children still need us to frame the world for them, to train them how to see and understand it. If we don't give them that framework, then books or television will, or their friends, or the internet. Throughout their lives, it is our blessing to answer the questions they may be thinking but are not openly asking yet. It's our job to get ahead of them and frame for them the questions and issues that may be coming next in their lives, instead of desperately trying to chase and chip into the perceptions that the world has already put in. We want our children to see the world through the framework we have helped them to shape in their minds.

Encounter God and his truth

While we may only be able to take an optician's approach, coaching our children from the outside, God himself can work with them from the inside. He created them and he is with them always. He knows what they are thinking. He knows what is in their hearts and he is daily developing them to be more like him. He is also speaking to them and acting in partnership with them in their spiritual and mental transformation. It is important for us, as parents, to keep that truth at the forefront of this process.

Another key tool is for us continually to coach our children to connect with God through scripture and through a heart-to-heart relationship with him. So much in our world shifts. When we help our children to ground themselves in the Bible, then they will have unshakeable access to truth. When we encourage and equip them to ground themselves in a vibrant, joy-filled relationship with God, then they will have unshakeable access to the love, healing and blessing of the Almighty.

Equip children to be powerful in shaping their own minds

Ultimately, each of us is responsible for the way we think and perceive, and we have a lifetime of opportunities in which we can continue to adjust our minds. After all, we are on a lifelong journey of personal transformation. While our children are in our homes, we can create tools for them to use, to help them adjust their thinking and perceptions on their own. Over time and with use, some of these tools will become a natural part of our children's own tool set. By the time they leave to live on their own, we want them to be fully equipped with a powerful arsenal of practised strategies that they can employ when life presents challenges. We want them to be able to assess themselves effectively and make changes, keep a God-centred mindset, adjust their plans when necessary, and continue to learn along their journey of personal transformation.

When I first had my glasses, I was not in the habit of wearing them. I began to discover that the cost of amazing vision was to remember my glasses, to take care of my glasses, and to actually wear my glasses. It was inconvenient at first, but after a while I didn't even think about it. I wouldn't even consider not wearing my glasses or my contact lenses now. It is one of the healthiest, most wonderful daily blessings I have. Once our children learn to see the fruit of a God-centred mindset in their lives, they will learn to value and embrace the cost of choosing to go on the journey of partnership with God in transforming their minds.

*

Section 3

Everyday applications

Chapter 7

Introduction to everyday applications

> God is awesome and holy, and he loves me totally and unreasonably.
>
> He is daily shaping me to be like him, and I am not finished yet.
>
> I am invited to be a small part of his wonderful plans.

When I was young, I thought that parenting was instinctive, that it would naturally flow out of me just the way I wanted. As I grew older I began to realise that rarely does anything good come out of me by pure instinct. The instinctive me is clunky and inconsistent and variable and selfish and, often, inflexible. Anything good I do has come out of a deliberate choice to make what is on my heart and mind bear fruit in my life and be reflected in my decisions and relationships. From pursuing health to trying to be a more gracious and loving boss, to giving my husband my best instead of my emotional leftovers, I must look at my life and the way I operate and I must choose to be the person I want to be.

Parenting for confidence is a choice. It requires us to step back for a moment, to look at our parenting and ask ourselves, 'Is this the way I want to do it? Is this producing the spiritual fruit in my children's lives that my heart longs for? Am I being who God has called me to be here? What do I need to change in myself and in my approach, so that my children can be truly confident?'

I can't tell you how many times I have read a parenting book and tried to pick up the suggestions, only to be annoyed that they didn't 'work' with my child or frustrated with myself when I couldn't remember the programme or stick with it. Chasing formulas is exhausting and disappointing, and it somehow feels disconnected from what's happening in our hearts. My goal is for you to feel that parenting for confidence can flow naturally from your heart.

In this section the chapters will:

- focus on a specific parenting moment and address its key questions
- take a deeper look at the issue
- put the tools of hearts and minds into action

Before we continue, here is a quick reminder of the tools we've covered in the 'Hearts' and 'Minds' chapters. Don't worry about remembering them. Throughout this section, I will specifically list the tools when they are put into action, so that you can see when they are used.

We will use these *tools for the heart* to help us draw close to our children's hearts.

- Understand through curiosity
- Respond with empathy and bring truth

- Connect children to yourself and God
- Help them to be powerful for the next time

We will use these *tools for the mind* to help us adjust our children's thinking.

- Direct attention and values
- Use foundational phrases
- Verbally frame what children are seeing
- Encounter God and his truth
- Equip children to be powerful in shaping their own minds

When we begin to parent out of our deep beliefs, then the pressure of doing everything 'just right' can fall away. We will become more bold and proactive as we choose to parent from our hearts, and the fruits of confidence will begin to grow in our children.

*

Chapter 8

Embrace the journey: who am I?

Key question: What do we do when our children concern themselves with asking, 'Who am I?'

One day I was walking across the park with Joseph, one of the young people from my church. He wanted to talk.

'Secondary school is different from what I thought it would be,' he said. 'People aren't mean. It's just...' He paused and nervously swept his hair across his forehead. 'Well... it's just that Mum keeps telling me to be myself. She says that if I'd just be myself, then people would like me for who I am. I feel like I'm supposed to know what that is. But I really don't. How can I be myself if I don't know who I'm supposed to be? Is that wrong?'

When our core of confidence centres on the belief that 'I must be confident, proud and bold in who I am', then the question 'But who am I?' becomes a huge one. Never before has there been such pressure on children and young people to be able to define themselves, to be able to describe and summarise who they are. The belief that we are all special and unique and should be able to express ourselves in a way that reflects our individuality thunders in their ears. The pressure on our children to prove their uniqueness can be stifling.

A deeper look at the issue

Society has rushed in to help us discover our uniqueness so that we can categorise ourselves and define ourselves clearly. There are countless personality tests, colour profiles, quizzes and categories for our children to discover themselves in. We see our children quickly jumping into these 'tests', seeking to understand who they are and to define themselves, because the demand of the world has fuelled their curiosity to discover and define who they are and who they are not.

Personality versus character

As we discussed before, there is a difference between personality and character. Personality is a hardwired instinct in our brains. For instance, when children are faced with something new, each child will react differently. One child may be naturally cautious, waiting for someone else to try the activity first, while another may be reckless, rushing right in before she has even looked at it properly. Broadly speaking, current research studies show that the personality we have in preschool is, essentially, the personality we will have for the rest of our lives. Personality can be changed, but it requires much conscious and deliberate effort on our parts.

While personality may affect how we initially feel in a scenario, character determines how we will respond to it. Character is something that we *can* shape. Character is about who we are in the moment, the combination of our past and our present, our hopes for the future, and the way we make decisions. We can teach our children to be brave in the face of something new, even if bravery is not their initial reaction. We can teach them skills to reduce their anxiety. We can teach them how to see a new situation so that it is no longer either terrifying or unreasonably attractive. We can teach them restraint, so that they assess the dangers before they jump. Character is constantly being moulded as we go through life because our life lessons and experiences constantly shape the way we choose to respond to situations and scenarios.

Too often we begin to muddle personality and character in our heads, and then our children become confused about them, too. They begin to view everything about themselves as permanent. They begin to believe that when they were born, they were born complete, and that their lives are simply a journey of understanding themselves better and better and learning to be confident in who they are. This confusion is damaging our children and stopping them from experiencing the freedom that God designed for them, because the truth is far different.

Limits within the box

By placing an increasing value on individuality, society has replaced the value of personal transformation with an emphasis on personally expressing what already exists. Inevitably, then, our children begin to see themselves as fixed, locked into who they are. They can begin to think, 'I was created in one way, and now that's it. I have to live within that realm of my personality.' Their journey becomes about expressing themselves where they are, as opposed to anticipating, with hope and joy and freedom of choice, the person they will be tomorrow. When our children view themselves as fixed, they accept both character flaws and weaknesses as part of their identity, and they don't see that these flaws can possibly be changed.

Our children often learn to see themselves in a box. They believe that in order to succeed in this world, they must define that box as quickly and as comprehensively as possible, and then they must defend the box vigorously.

- I am good at maths. I am not good at reading or writing.
- I am sporty and funny. I am not clever.
- I hate being in charge. I love serving.
- I say it like it is, and that's just me.

They then conclude, 'I must be a pastoral, sporty, fun-loving girl who could get only these types of jobs and serve in these areas of church,' and they reject everything that doesn't fit in their boxes. 'Oh no, I couldn't do that. It's just not "me"'; 'I couldn't speak at the front. It's just not "me"'; 'I couldn't write a book. I have dyslexia. It's not "me".'

But when we think in terms of possibilities for change, there are no limits on how God can use us. There is nothing for us to argue with God about. We will be able to respond to him like this: 'I am me, and God loves me. If he's asking me to do this, then I will do it, because he knows me way better than I know myself.'

When you ask your child to do something you know he is capable of, do you want to stop and have a debate with him about whether or not it fits with his personality? Do you want your requests to be restricted, based on what he thinks his limitations are? You know your children well, and you want them to be living in the fullness of who they are. You may know better than they do what that is.

How much more does our Father know the depths of the personality, skills and giftings he's put in each of us, and how our character is being developed at any given moment.

Freedom outside the box

If it's not important for our children to know what 'boxes' they fit in, to be able to answer God's call, why push them to pursue that knowledge? Of what benefit are the boxes? If we never focus our children's attention on the boxes, but instead encourage them to focus on the fact that they are loved totally by a great God who is asking them to do powerful things today and tomorrow, then our children can begin to respond to their heart and to God's heart without the walls of a box blocking them in.

If we refuse to accept our children's boxes, we prevent our children from placing their confidence in themselves, in their own definitions of who they are. If God asks me to speak at a conference, I could respond, 'Yes, I can do that. I'm good at it. I am a teacher and a preacher. I am funny and people really enjoy laughing at my talks. Not a problem. Yes, God, I will do that.' Or I could respond, 'Thank you, God, for choosing me to do this thing with you. Thank you for what you want to say to these people and for the joy I will get in doing this with you. Absolutely, yes!' In both cases, I accept the speaking engagement, but where I place my confidence is radically different in each case.

I love the way God declared himself to Moses. Moses stood before the burning bush and asked, 'What is your name?' God answered, 'I Am Who I Am' (Exodus 3:13–14). He didn't rattle off a list of traits showing who he was. At that moment he didn't hyper-define himself. His initial response to Moses was to say that his name was 'I Am'. You see, God is the ultimate everything, and so the most powerful, most complete description he could use was simply 'I Am'.

Wouldn't it be great for our children to be so comfortable and confident that it is enough for them to wake up every day and think 'I am just me'? No limits; no boxes; secure in the knowledge that they are totally and completely loved by an amazing God, by the great 'I Am'. Then they would be free to laugh and be silly, to like what they like and be good at what they're good at. They can hope in the future and not be limited by their self-imposed boxes. They can embrace the journey of letting God develop and transform them, and they can experience the joy and freedom that comes with being in the middle of it all. They can acknowledge their weaknesses and failings and be aware that they are not yet all they want to be. They can feel unashamed to get help and to grow. They can delight in the everyday incompleteness of themselves, knowing that their 'now' is good and their future is glorious because their God is faithful.

The danger of labels

If we want our children to live free from a box, we must be careful not to attempt to create one for them. When we tell our children who they are, we may want them to take our words on as part of their identity: 'You are wonderful, beautiful, funny and clever.' We want them to define themselves by the labels we create for them. We want them to believe those things about themselves and to be confident in them. We believe that our job as parents is to help our children define themselves in a positive way. What happens, though, is that when we construct an identity like this for our children—a box for them to cling to and live in—that identity becomes a fragile core that they must contain. If we tell them, 'You are unique; you are perfect; you are funny and beautiful and clever', then we are setting them up for a battle. What happens to their confidence when they find that someone else doesn't think that way about them—when someone criticises them or says hurtful things? What happens to their confidence when we have told them they are unique and special, and then someone else comes along with the same traits or skills? What happens when their 'uniqueness' isn't unique any more? It shatters them. It makes them question everything about themselves because their trust was in their labels.

In our effort to help our children form a good self-image, we essentially judge them and then ask them to adopt our judgements. We have watched and assessed them, and then we declare, 'Yes, according to me and the world, you can be classed as clever. Here you go—accept this label. Put it in your box.' So our child does as we say. Later on, though, someone else comes along and says, 'I disagree. You are stupid. Here you go—accept this label. Put it in your box.' So our child puts that one in his box, too. Eventually it becomes a battle of the labels, a battle between the influences that shout ever louder, 'You are this! You are that!' Sadly, we often lose the battle.

God's approach is different. Remember what God said to Moses when Moses wanted an affirmation of his own identity (Exodus 4:11–12)? Remember what Jesus said to the woman at the well? He spoke about himself (John 4:14). When we connect our children to God, he shows them who he is and he whispers his love for them. He connects with them heart to heart and draws them to his heart, instead of shouting one more label into the cacophony of labels bombarding them.

How can we lay a foundation in God so that our children can develop their core of confidence in him and not in themselves?

Putting the 'hearts and minds' tools into action

Here are a few suggestions to get you started in building a core of confidence.

> God is awesome and holy, and he loves me totally and unreasonably.
> He is daily shaping me to be like him, and I am not finished yet.
> I am invited to be a small part of his wonderful plans.

Affirm children through relationship, not through labels

- Hearts: Connect children to yourself
- Minds: Use foundational phrases; verbal framing

Truth is in the relationship. I believe I'm funny because people laugh, not because people tell me I'm funny. I believe my mum loves me because I see it in her actions, her eyes and her hugs, so when she says that she loves me, I believe it. If we change our language, so that we are affirming our children through relationship, we will build in them a freedom to be loved and to be 'I am' in our presence. We will build in our children a relationship where they can see who they are, reflected in how others react to their character. Today they may love playing the trombone, and tomorrow they may love bowling. Through it all, as they tell us stories of their lives and the worries of their hearts, we can affirm them on their journey.

Try communicating encouragement, love and approval to your children in ways that emphasise your relationship with them and their effect on you, instead of pushing them to accept the label you want them to embrace. For instance, avoid starting sentences with 'You are…' or 'You look…', such as 'You are so smart. You are so clever. You are so funny. You look so beautiful. You are so creative.'

Instead, describe how you are affected by who they are or what they do—for example, 'I love watching how you do [xxxx]. I love [xxxx] about you. When we are together, I feel [xxxx]. When you do [xxxx], I feel [xxxx].'

There is such a difference between 'You are loved' and 'I love you with all my heart'. There is such a difference between 'You are funny' and 'I love laughing with you. Days with you are filled with fun'. There is such a difference between 'You are beautiful' and 'I feel such joy when I am with you. I admire you so much'. There is such a difference between 'You are clever' and 'I love the way your mind works'.

If we do this well, our daughter won't agonise about whether random strangers think her body is beautiful or not, because she will know that her family and friends cherish her heart and delight in her presence. She will be better able to decide whom she wants to be with and what relationships are healthy for her, because she already sees how she positively affects those close to her and how others have a positive effect on her. She can wisely choose to be in relationships where people deeply value, protect and cherish her.

If we do it well, our son won't be desperately focused on trying to live out labels, because he will know that we love everything about him. We delight in his company. He brings us joy and laughter. He makes our hearts feel full with love. Our favourite parts of the day are when we get to hear his thoughts and play with him, and when we get to share our hearts about things we feel and think. Not everyone is going to feel that way about our sons—but we do, and God does.

Talk about transformation and share your stories

- Hearts: Connect children to yourself and God
- Minds: Direct attention; equip children to be powerful; encounter God and his truth

When we make our core of confidence about God, then we begin to grasp that we have not finished growing yet and that God invites us, every day, to be a small part of his great plan. We begin to realise that who I am today isn't who I am going to be tomorrow, because God is shaping me and I'm helping him to do so. Labels don't fit because we are constantly changing.

Create a culture in your home where changing, learning and improving are regularly celebrated, discussed and expected. Talk about what you are learning at school or work. Share stories of how you are changing in response to scripture or circumstances. Share what you and God have been talking about. Apologise when you need to, and discuss what it's like to be on your own journey of transformation. In this way, as I've mentioned before, you create windows into your own life with God. Invite people over for dinner who have great stories of meeting God and can explain how having him in their lives has made a radical difference.

Talk about labels that you have believed about yourself, and how you are on a journey of realising that your core of confidence has been misplaced. Have conversations about characters in movies and on television who constantly talk about themselves and about 'being themselves'. Wonder why they say that, and invite your child into a conversation about it.

Read Bible stories with your child, focusing on people who had a good core of confidence and whom God took on a journey of transformation. Discuss the changes in the disciples and in characters such as Esther and Joseph, and notice how God continued to develop them throughout their lives.

At night, spend time with your child chatting with God about your days and what you have been thinking. Invite God to shape your characters and hearts to be more like him. The more we can make our home a place where we can all delight in the middle stages of our process of transformation, the more our children will learn to embrace each stage of their growth in God.

*

— Chapter 9 —

Encouraging for confidence

Key question: How do we encourage our children if we no longer use labels?

Our children believe that we value the things we praise. They hear how we praise them, and they think that what we praise most, we value most. I would suggest that most of us haven't thought much about what qualities we praise.

A deeper look at the issue

We often praise what is before our eyes—the most obvious thing. Often we encourage our children without thinking. They come down for church dressed well and we praise the way they look: 'You are beautiful'; 'What a handsome little man.' They win a competition and we praise their achievement: 'Well done! You won!' We praise their obedience: 'Good boy!'

I would suggest that we have been taught to praise these things, maybe by the world or maybe by our own parents. We praise children because we want them to feel confident; we want to build their self-esteem. The problem is that our praise isn't always an accurate reflection of our parenting values. For me, the three most important traits I would want to see in my child are not the ones above—looking good, winning and being obedient—but they are the qualities we unconsciously end up praising. Think about it. What do you praise the most in your home?

The world says we must 'be' many things, so we strive to meet those standards, but our insecurity and pain illuminate our wounds when we feel that we don't measure up. We end up defeated and say, 'I guess I'm ugly' or 'I'm not that funny'. Then, as Christians, we hear these words and rush in to fill the hole. 'Yes, it's important to be beautiful and funny!' we say to ourselves. 'In God's eyes you *are* those things. Ignore what those mean people say. Ignore what you say to yourself. To God you *are* beautiful and funny. Feel confident! You *are* all those things, just by being you.'

Actually, though, when we look closely at what the world says is important, all those things don't amount to much. They are just worldly judgements and worldly values. In the end, most of them don't matter—at all.

What matters to God? What traits are the core of the way he sees us? Our heart. Our holiness and righteousness in him. Our decisions. Our humility. Our love.

Instead of praising according to the world's measuring sticks, what if we encouraged and praised in accordance with what God has called us to? What would it look like if we deliberately praised our children for the traits we really want to see growing in them? What if we praised our children not for the things we see on the surface but for the deeper values we want to see in their lives?

The following is not a comprehensive list; it just happens to be my list. It's a sampling of the character traits I see valued in scripture, so I often talk about these traits when I'm with children. Each of us will have different values we cherish from the Bible, so your list may not look the same as mine. That's OK!

These are the traits I want to see in my child:

- Love of learning
- Ability to see opportunity in failure and to bounce back easily
- Curiosity
- Deep compassion
- Love
- Joy
- Peace
- Patience
- Kindness
- Mercy
- Grace
- Humility
- Goodness
- Gentleness
- Faithfulness
- Self-control
- Courage
- Sacrifice
- Generosity
- Love of being on a team and ability to value others' contributions
- Wisdom
- Boldness

- Bravery
- Justice
- Perseverance
- Problem-solving ability
- Ability to be a good friend
- Honesty

Note that this isn't a gendered list. It is a list of character traits that God calls us all to develop, no matter what our gender. It is important that we praise our boys for their kindness and self-control as much as we praise our girls for those same traits. Similarly, we should praise our girls for bravery and sacrifice as much as we praise our boys. All of these character traits reflect Christ, and we are each called to be like him.

When we stop or greatly reduce our praise of the superficial, such as cleverness, beauty, physical strength, politeness or being good at something, and start praising the biblical character traits and truths we see in our children, then those traits will begin to develop and blossom.

I want my child to be confident that he can control himself and his emotions, that he can be powerfully courageous and filled with joy each day. I want him to flourish in progressing with his maths, even if he isn't at the top of his set. I want him to see the power of his gentleness with others each day. If I want all of this, I have to start showing him that these things are important to me and to him.

For some of us, this will take a huge mind shift and, most of all, a change in our habits. When I started, I was amazed at how many platitudes I was throwing at my child, how many superficial things I was praising. I had to learn to look for and praise a different set of qualities.

Putting the 'hearts and minds' tools into action

Here are a few suggestions to get you started in building a core of confidence.

> God is awesome and holy, and he loves me totally and unreasonably.
> He is daily shaping me to be like him, and I am not finished yet.
> I am invited to be a small part of his wonderful plans.

Pause to reflect

- Minds: Use foundational phrases

Take some time to listen to yourself. If you do nothing else this week, just pay attention to what you are saying when you praise your children. Some of us are effusive parents, praising everything all the time. Some of us have fallen into the trap of praising with the phrases we've always used. Perhaps we don't actually praise our children very often at all, and we may need to look at ways we can increase our praise.

If it would help, jot down the phrases you say most when you encourage and praise your children. Circle the phrases you like, and put a big X through the ones you want to replace. Do you agree with the phrases still on your list? Are those your values? Could you be any more specific about the ones you like? Could you tell stories about them? Maybe you could ask your children more questions to push further into those areas of encouragement that you have already identified as important.

Brainstorm your own list of key character traits you want to develop in your child. Use your Bible and your knowledge of God's character as the basis for your list, or you are likely to end up using the world's values instead. Keep in mind that your list will change as your child grows and matures. Once you have created your list, pick out a few traits you would like to start working on right away.

Give specific praise

- Minds: Verbal framing

Create some affirming phrases and try them out, so that you will have them ready to use when the opportunity arises. Here are a few examples.

- Great effort! That is so kind!
- Wonderful perseverance. You never gave up!
- I saw you were getting angry, and then you kept control of your body and words and didn't hurt anyone, even though you were angry.

- You were so courageous today. When you went up on to that stage, you looked even braver than David from the story of David and Goliath!

Try to stay away from labels. Instead of saying, 'What a kind boy', try saying, 'That was so kind.' Instead of saying, 'You are so good', try 'I love seeing how you keep choosing goodness every day.' The fewer labels children have to carry, the more confident they can be in their capacity to change and to become better tomorrow than they are today.

Give feedback

- Minds: Direct attention
- Hearts: Connect children to yourself; respond with empathy and truth

Our children are doing great work all the time, and they are powerful people who have an impact on others. Don't just praise them when an event happens. Notice when your children are exhibiting character traits that make you proud, and feed back to them how their actions affect you and others:

- Thank you so much for telling me you love me. When you do that, it makes me feel so warm and happy inside.
- You are always so quick to share your treats. It makes me want to share, too. Thank you for being generous.
- I know I can count on you to have your seatbelt buckled before I start the car. I really appreciate your faithfulness. It makes me feel as if we are a team.

Ask questions

- Hearts: Understand through curiosity; respond with empathy and truth

The questions we ask our children reveal what we consider to be important. Of course we want to find out what happened at school today, but we can ask other questions, too:

- What made you really happy today?
- Was there anyone lonely or lost who you managed to help?
- What was the worst part of your day? What was the best?
- Did anything worry you?
- How is your best friend feeling?
- Can you tell me a story of someone who needed your kindness today?

Tell stories

- Hearts: Connect children to yourself
- Minds: Verbal framing

So often, our children only hear us tell stories of their misdeeds or the funny things they have done. Hero stories are a feast for children, whether the stories come from the Bible, books or television programmes. Our children aspire to be heroes, so begin to tell stories in which your child is the hero. I've found that the car is a great place to do this.

Once upon a time, there was Sophia, and she was at gymnastics class working really hard. Up she jumped to the balance beam, and then—ooops—she fell off! Sophia fell off over and over again, but did she give up? No, she did not. She kept trying. Up she went again, and this time she went a bit farther, but then—oh, no! Off again. What should she do? Should she scream and cry? Should she get angry? Should she stomp away? Did she give up? No, she did not! She kept trying and learning and getting better and better! Woo-hoo! Go, Sophie!

Honey, did I tell you about what Sakib did today? I was feeling tired when we got home so I flopped on the couch. Then my son, who I love, said, 'Mummy, you look tired. Do you want to read a book?' and he brought me a book before he went to play in his room. I felt so taken care of. I was so blessed by Sakib's kind and caring heart.

Our children need to know that we see the deep character that is growing inside them and that we celebrate and care about it.

*

— Chapter 10 —

Media and the world's messages

Key questions: Our children live in a broken world, which has values and standards very far from God's design. How do I as a parent build healthy, powerful foundations for my children so that they can face the world's assaults with confidence? How do I train my children to engage with the wrongness of the world's messages? What skills and tools do I need to give them so that they can recentre their core of confidence by themselves?

A deeper look at the issue

When we talk about this topic, we often use the phrase 'in the world but not of the world'. It's a summary of Jesus' words in the Gospel of John, when he prayed for his followers before he died on the cross (see John 17:14–19). It has come to mean something quite specific to us: we are to live in this world, which holds ideals so different from ours, and yet we are not to own those ideals or to let those standards rule us.

When we look at an issue such as how the world is influencing our children, we feel stressed partly because we see the destructive nature of the world and we want to protect our children from it. We don't want them to be growing up with body-image issues or shame about their lack of skill in one area or another. We don't want them to feel alone or the odd one out.

I think we have to remember God's goal for us—a deep relationship with him that brings us love and joy, personal transformation and a daily purpose with him. God does not guarantee us an easy and perfect life on earth.

Jesus spoke clearly to his followers about what life would be like for them on earth. He taught them that 'in this world you will have trouble' (John 16:33) and he explained to them why 'the world hates you' (15:18). He was preparing his followers for difficulty because life would not be easy for them. Over the decades after Jesus' resurrection, many of his followers were imprisoned, beaten, attacked, shipwrecked, yelled at and chased out of town, and some were even martyred. Others stayed in their own villages, raising families under oppression and abuse. I would propose that even through all these hardships, many of them persevered and committed themselves to living lives full of God's love, peace, purpose and joy. They established deep, supportive communities and they saw their numbers increase as more people were healed and transformed, even while facing persecution. These early Christians didn't have easy lives, isolated from the world, yet they lived in fullness of life in the midst of their fearful and evil world for the purposes of God's glory. We want that kind of fullness of life for our children today.

Isolation from the world isn't God's goal for our children. God wants them to experience the freedom and goodness that come from having him at the core of their confidence while living in the midst of a broken world that needs him.

So how do we train our children to be purposeful in the world and operate boldly from a God-centred core of confidence? How do we raise our children to be 'in the world but not of it'?

I would suggest that:

- We *build* a healthy and powerful foundation for our children by raising them with a solid foundation of God's truth.
- We *empower* them with the skills and wisdom to look at the world and see the unhealthy and warped messages and standards that are being sold to them.
- We *equip* them to monitor and feed their own hearts and minds so they can continue to adjust themselves and stay close to God throughout a lifetime of being bombarded by media and the world's standards.

Let's look at how we can do all of this by using the 'hearts and minds' tools.

Putting the 'hearts and minds' tools into action

Here are a few suggestions to get you started in building a core of confidence in your children.

Building foundations

How do we build healthy, powerful foundations for our children so that they can face the world's assault with confidence? We do it by raising our children with a solid foundation of God's truth.

Understand God's standard

- Minds: Encounter God and his truth; use foundational phrases; verbal framing

If we are going to empower our children to live according to God's standards and messages, our children need to know what they are. Scripture is full of God's direction for our lives, but Jesus boils it down to one concept for us—love. While the world is shouting about power, success, wealth and self-fulfilment, Jesus speaks about love.

'As the Father has loved me, so have I loved you. Now remain in my love.' (John 15:9)

'"Love the Lord your God with all your heart and with all your soul and with all your mind." This is the first and greatest commandment. And the second is like it: "Love your neighbour as yourself." All the Law and the Prophets hang on these two commandments.' (Matthew 22:37–40)

Love is the centre of God's plan and God's messages. Because God is at the centre of our core of confidence, his love is at its very root.

> God is awesome and holy, and he loves me totally and unreasonably.
>
> He is daily shaping me to be like him, and I am not finished yet.
>
> I am invited to be a small part of his wonderful plans.

God's wonderful plans are for the world to be reunited with his love. His love draws us in, transforms us and powerfully seeks all those who are far from him.

The world's values are reflections of a world far from perfect love, a world full of sin. Without God's perfect love, our world is filled with fear, selfishness, pain and loneliness.

Our role as children of God is to live lives of love and to bring his love into every situation we can. As our children learn that God's love is to be at the centre of their lives and that it is also the guide for their lives, then they can begin to learn how to be in the world but not of it. They will learn to see the difference that God's love can make in a lost and dying world, and they will learn how to walk with God's love into a land that is desperate for it.

Our lives are journeys of learning to love God and others in the fullness of the way he has loved us, and we can coach our children along the road. Children will need to learn how to connect with God's love and, especially, how to love others safely and well. They will need to grow in understanding the boundaries of love and the disciplines of choosing love when it is illogical or undeserved.

Begin to frame for your children that God is all about love, showing them how the centre of his way of life for us is to be loved by him, to love him in return and to love others. As you read the newspaper at breakfast or watch the news in the evening together, chat about the way the world is broken because God and his love are no longer at the centre of people's lives. Many people don't know God's love, so they don't make decisions based on his love for them or his love for others. They hurt each other and strive for power or success or anything else that they think will fill the hole in their lives.

You can chat about how, even in our lives, when we get stressed or worried it's because we forget how wonderful God is and how he loves us. We snap at each other when we get tired because we forget to show how much we love each other. When we forget love, life doesn't work the way it is supposed to.[3]

Create experiences that put God's love into action

- Hearts: Connect children to yourself and God
- Minds: Encounter God and his truth; direct attention and values

Often our children see God's instructions for life as rules and restrictions instead of blessings and powerful life patterns. When we create experiences for our children that put God's love into action, we give them a deeper understanding of God's heart and of the fruit that grows when we act through his love.

Rather than saying, 'We need to take care of the poor', create opportunities for your children to do so. You might take them to a homeless shelter and help to serve meals, or you might go to a food bank and help to distribute food. Before you start out, talk about how God loves each person as much as he loves us. God specifically tells us that he is close to those in need and he wants us to serve them well. In fact, he says that whatever we do for them is the same as doing it directly for Jesus (Matthew 25:40). After you have served together, discuss what is happening in your children's hearts and minds. Discuss why God's heart is toward the poor and why he delights in our service to them. Discuss other ways in which people can be poor, not just in terms of financial need. What would it look like to love them? What would it look like to love those in need at school?

Such experiences don't have to involve a trip, and they don't have to be a big deal. They can be simple. Children can put God's love into action by serving alongside us at church. Within our homes, we can create opportunities for them to pray for other family members. No matter where you are, look for opportunities for your children to experience the power and fruit of God's love in action. As they begin to see how kindness, grace, service and love affect people powerfully, the pull that the world's values have on their lives will begin to diminish.

When Jesus was praying to his Father for us before he died, he said:

I have given them your teaching. And the world has hated them, because they don't belong to the world, just as I don't belong to the world. I am not asking you to take them out of the world but to keep them safe from the Evil One. They don't belong to the world, just as I don't belong to the world. Make them ready for your service through your truth; your teaching is truth. I have sent them into the world, just as you sent me into the world. For their sake, I am making myself ready to serve so that they can be ready for their service of the truth. (John 17:14–19, NCV)

The whole point of being 'not of the world' is that we can go into it and serve its people well, and we can declare God's truth in it well. If our children never learn the power of his love, his truth and his way, they will not feel inspired to live according to these qualities.

Discover the stories of God's people

• Minds: Direct attention; encounter God and his truth

Stories are among the most powerful tools we have for transmitting culture and understanding values. Our children need to be surrounded by the true stories of people like themselves who have lived lives of love, who have had a core of confidence that enabled them to be 'in the world but not of the world'.

Read Bible stories together, paying particular attention to the way people walked with God, living according to his standards in a world that was different. Read about Shadrach, Meshach and Abednego (Daniel 1—3), Daniel in the lions' den (Daniel 6), Joseph serving Potiphar in a faraway land (Genesis 39), Paul ministering to people who wanted to kill him (Acts 21), and Jesus eating with sinners (Mark 2:13–17). Look not only at the lives of the well-known disciples but also at the many lesser-named or unnamed followers of Christ who barely get a mention—men and women who were steadfast in serving God, despite their hardships (see 2 Corinthians 6:3–10). Their stories are also valuable. For example, I think of the seven servants chosen in Acts 6, the men and women dragged away and imprisoned by Saul, the ones who helped Saul escape in a basket, Ananias in Damascus, Lydia in Philippi, and Jason in Thessalonica. Scripture is rich with people from ordinary places who faced being 'in the world but not of it'.

Expose your children to stories of historical and modern-day heroes of the faith, such as Eric Liddell, Corrie Ten Boom, Miep Gies, Irena Sendler, Nate Saint and Elisabeth Elliot, to name a few. They are inspirations for us all. Hear testimonies of modern missionaries and of people in your local church who daily try to live lives of love while they are 'in the world', including teachers, waitresses, council workers, doctors, lawyers and school children.

The more examples our children have of people who make a difference because they know how to live 'in the world' without being 'of the world', the more clearly they will see how to walk boldly with God's love into the toughest places of their own everyday lives.

Serpents and doves

How do we train our children to engage with the wrongness of the world's messages? We empower them with the skills and wisdom necessary to see the unhealthy, warped values that the world tries to sell to them.

When Jesus sent out his twelve disciples to start ministering, he said to them, 'I am sending you out like sheep among wolves. Therefore be as shrewd as snakes and as innocent as doves' (Matthew 10:16). He was sending his disciples into a hostile and hurting world, and his advice to them was to be both wise and innocent. He wanted his disciples to walk in love and accomplish the purpose he sent them for, but to do so gently and wisely. It was Jesus' strategy for them to be in the world but not of it.

Let's explore some of the 'hearts and minds' tools that our children need in order to be wise about the world and yet to respond to it well.

Spot the lie

- Hearts: Understand through curiosity
- Minds: Direct attention; verbal framing; equip children to be powerful in shaping their own minds

The world's messages are subtle, creeping into our children's minds and hearts through advertising, television, casual conversation and games. The power of subtlety is that the message slides in without our knowledge. One of the significant things we can do to counter it is to shine a light on the strategies the world uses to send lies our way. We can make our home a place of glaring truth and equip our children to see the lies for themselves.

For instance, you can expose the techniques that the

world uses to promote its destructive values, from product placement (where companies pay to have characters on TV and movies using their products, so that we think they're cool) to computer retouching of photos in magazines. Ask 'Did you know?' questions and drop titbits of useful information into your conversations as the facts pop into your head, when you watch TV or when you see an advert on the side of the bus. Watch YouTube videos that show how models are made to look more muscular or thin than they really are. Question the plot lines in movies.

You can also laugh at the lies. Make a game out of it, declaring them not to be true. So many times, the world's messages go unchallenged as they enter our homes. Don't just let them slide in; instead, highlight what is wrong and laugh at messages that are lies or make no sense. Play a game of how many untrue things you can find on adverts as you walk down the high street. Challenge the logos and photos, saying, 'What? That's crazy!'

One afternoon, my husband Mark and I were at a restaurant with our then three-year-old son. Mark leaned across the table and picked up the kids' entertainment pack that my son had been given to colour. 'Caleb, look at this!' he said. 'There's something very silly on this paper. What is the difference between the boy picture and the girl picture?'

Caleb scrunched up his face and analysed the pictures hard, but he couldn't find any difference.

My husband pointed to the drawing of a girl. 'Look,' he said. 'They drew her body super-small, much smaller than the boy's! How silly is that?'

I looked at the pictures and was surprised to see how

different they were. The girl's body was half the width of the boy's, even though their heads and feet were the same size.

Caleb's eyes widened. 'Girls don't look like that! How silly!' Then he started to giggle. 'She would break like that!'

'Hmm… well, what could we do?' Mark sat back in his chair and watched Caleb think.

'I can make her right,' he said, and then he added width and muscles to the girl's picture. 'Silly draw-ers.'

From adverts to television to books and toy packaging, there are so many lies that we can expose, debunk and laugh at. There is even a Twitter hashtag, #notbuyingit, dedicated to enabling people all over the world to voice their disagreement with the dangerous expectations outlined in movies and advertising. What would it look like if our children grew up identifying the unhealthy values portrayed around them and simply dismissing them?

Try shining a light on destructive values in the media. Sometimes our children need to see how to apply God's love to something that seems innocuous, like a television show. What if they heard you say something like this: 'I really don't like this programme, because it wants us to laugh at other people. Look at those contestants! They have hoped and dreamed for years for an opportunity like this, and then they've practised for days and waited in a queue for hours. I think they are brave and should be given respect and honour for their efforts. I don't think I want to laugh at them, and I don't like it when they're treated like that.'

Your words could open up a significant conversation with your family, and together you can decide how to move forward. So many television shows portray all sorts of assumptions that are not the truth—for example, that muscular men are the only ones who are attractive to women, that children are expected to be rude to their parents, or that siblings will inevitably hate each other. Television shows give us assumptions about life and values and ask us to accept them. Some of them are true, but, with those assumptions that are false, we have a marvellous opportunity to shine a light on the lies.

Engage with fiction, keeping God's love and values in mind

- Hearts: Understand through curiosity; respond with empathy and bring truth
- Minds: Verbal framing; encounter God and his truth

The question we have to ask ourselves is this: what stories surround our children and what are these stories telling them? There are very few stories in the world that fully embrace all of our values, and that is OK. Most stories present a combination of values that we agree and disagree with. As parents, we need to decide which stories we allow into our home and how we are going to engage with their content.

An example of this is the 'Harry Potter' series, which centres on a child who lives in a world of magic and attends a school that teaches him magic. An evil wizard arises and the seven books outline the story of a battle against this wizard and his terrible army. Many Christian parents came out quite strongly against the series, not allowing their children to read the books or watch the films that came later. Other Christian parents read the books with their children, discussing them along the way. Others saw nothing wrong with the stories and allowed their children to read and watch them freely, discussing them as plot points came up in conversation. I have my opinion, and I'm sure you have yours, but I mention it because things like this happen all the time. From old Disney movies to the most modern Pixar films, stories are flooding towards our children, and we must choose how we want to engage with those stories.

Choosing not to let your children watch or read something is absolutely fine, and it gives you a good opportunity to explain why. When I was a child, my mum refused to let me see the musical *Grease* until I was a teenager. She told me repeatedly that she didn't like the way the leading girl character changed her values at the end, and that it wasn't worth the money or the time to watch the film. Eventually, when I was a teenager, we did go to see a performance of *Grease* at a local theatre. By then, I definitely understood what my mum had been talking about, and I agreed with her that it was not a happy ending for the girl, because she had compromised her values and her integrity for a guy.

Please don't misunderstand me: stories are to be enjoyed and delighted in. Read books for fun; watch movies to laugh. Please don't turn into the parent who has to have a conversation about everything, before, during and after every story or movie. You know which stories will make for interesting conversations about values and choices, so open up conversations about them.

Ask questions. What is the character thinking? Would

you do that? Why? Is that the way the world works? Why? Should it? What would you do in that situation? Who are you most like? Is that right? Wait a minute, a good character just did a bad thing; is that OK? Wait, a bad character did a good thing; does that mean he's not bad? Are people either good or bad? If this story were real, what would God be doing? Stories unlock our hearts and allow our children to find similarities between their own journeys and a character's, and to find differences between them, too. They can be powerful tools for exploring actions, choices and consequences.

It isn't just controversial stories that can give us interesting discussion opportunities. Even our most basic stories can open up some wonderful heart conversations with our children. The plot line of 'Goldilocks and the Three Bears' brings up an interesting thought: basically, the story is about a crime of breaking and entering. How did the bears feel? Why did Goldilocks feel it was OK to go in? Why wasn't she ever just content and grateful?

Look at some traditional Disney movies. How are leaders and royalty often portrayed? How do they use their powers? Take, for instance, the movie *Aladdin*. The sultan is an idiot and his chancellor is power-hungry. The basis for the plot is that there is an unjust law requiring a woman to marry before her 21st birthday. When the sultan's daughter rejects marriage, instead of changing the crazy law he allows her to become a pawn in a power game. What would your child do in that situation if they were the sultan? What is God's plan for bringing justice through leaders? These conversations are great for those bored-in-the-car moments when you can explore all angles of a well-known story or movie. The car is also a great place to discuss songs: 'Hey, I was thinking about that song we were singing and the words are kind of funny! What do they mean?'

Empowering children to recentre on their own

What skills and tools do we need to give our children so that they can recentre their core of confidence by themselves? We can equip them with tools to monitor and feed their own hearts and minds, so that they can continue to adjust themselves and stay close to God through a lifetime of bombardment by media and the world's standards.

Give children windows into your life in the world

- Hearts: Connect children to yourself and God; help them be powerful for the next time

You are perfectly positioned to show your children not only who God is but also who he is in relationship with a person— with you—which is so important. You can give them a peek into your own life with God. After all, you are the greatest resource your children will ever have. Daily, you model for them what is funny, what is terrifying, how to behave in a restaurant or on the beach, how to cope with anger or hurt. They are watching you. Unfortunately, we most often process our life with God silently, in our hearts and minds; our children are left guessing about how to do life with God, because we don't show them. One really powerful thing we can do is to create windows into our lives so that our children can see how we live with God. You don't need to share everything with them; this isn't a full disclosure policy. Just get into the pattern of regularly letting your children hear what is going on in your head and heart.

Life with God is about relationship with him and our purpose on earth. As our children grow, it is helpful for them to see that there is a difference between what we choose when we are close to God and what the world chooses. It is helpful for them to see how we negotiate being 'in the world but not of the world', and where God is in the process.

Create windows to allow your children to see a little of your journey of faith and decision-making when you are faced with a conflict of values. For example: 'Today I was at work, and my boss publicly said some really rude stuff about one of my colleagues. Everyone laughed really nervously, but I just froze. I felt that it was hurtful to my colleague, and not right. I thought I could either stay quiet, say something there, or confront my boss about it later. I ended up respectfully defending the man, and my boss wasn't pleased at all. I just couldn't let my boss's cruel words stand. Everyone needs someone to stand by them.'

Share stories with them of how the media affect you and what you do about it: 'I just can't watch *Britain's Next Top Model* any more. I spent so much time looking at myself in the mirror after that. How ridiculous! No more *Top Model* for me.' Explain the choices you make and how they help you live with integrity according to what you feel God is asking you to do. Invite your children to watch how you choose to be 'in the world', to hear how God speaks to you, guides you and encourages you, and to understand why you do what you do.

Help children monitor their own roots

- Hearts: Understand through curiosity; respond with empathy and bring truth; connect children to yourself and God; help them be powerful for the next time
- Minds: Equip children to be powerful in shaping their own minds

Each of us is responsible for our core, for what is in our hearts. As our children grow, one of our goals is to help them learn to reflect on what is going on in their own hearts so that they can adjust themselves with God and can keep their hearts right.

In Chapter 5, 'Hearts', we looked at tools to help us draw out our children through questions and through speaking truth into deep places. As our children grow, it's also helpful to teach them to do this for themselves. How can they notice what is going on in their heart's root system? How do they fix it? Jesus once said:

'Each tree is known by its own fruit... Good people bring good things out of the good they stored in their hearts. But evil people bring evil things out of the evil they stored in their hearts. People speak the things that are in their hearts.' (Luke 6:44–45, NCV)

I often tell children that one of their best clues to what is going on in their hearts is to listen to their own words. Are you complaining or whining a lot? Are you saying that you are scared or annoyed, or that you are fat, or that you want to be like someone else? Take a second to ponder what you are feeling underneath, that makes you so angry or worried, and start to bring some truth into your feelings. What does God's word say about your need or situation? Remind yourself of God's words. Remind yourself of his truth.

As parents, we can begin this process by reflecting our children's words back to them and coaching them through the reflective process. We might say, 'I noticed that every day this week you have used the word "stupid" about school. What's going on in your heart, that the word "stupid" keeps coming out? Just wondering'; or, 'You keep saying that you can't do this maths. You know that's not true about you, right? What is true?'

Sometimes the hurts that these words reveal need to be brought to God. We can also coach our children through the process of chatting with God about our hearts and of inviting him to come and heal, love, and fill our broken places and to communicate his wisdom and words to us.

Remain in God

- Hearts: Connect children to God; help them be powerful for the next time

Jesus said:

'If the world hates you, remember that it hated me first. If you belonged to the world, it would love you as it loves its own. But I have chosen you out of the world, so you don't belong to it. That is why the world hates you... They will do all this to you on account of me, because they do not know the One who sent me.' (John 15:18–19, 21, NCV)

We can often get wrapped up in defending ourselves against a world that hates us, and we worry about how to protect our children from that sting of hatred. When we pull back and take a wider look at John 15, we can see that right *before* Jesus talks about the world's hatred, he gives his disciples a strategy, a way for them to sustain themselves in him. He tells them this:

'I am the vine, and you are the branches. If any remain in me and I remain in them, they produce much fruit. But without me they can do nothing... I loved you as the Father loved me. Now remain in my love. I have obeyed my Father's commands, and I remain in his love. In the same way, if you obey my commands, you will remain in my love. I have told you these things so that you can have the same joy I have and so that your joy will be the fullest possible joy. This is my command: Love each other as I have loved you. The greatest love a person can show is to die for his friends.' (John 15:5, 9–13, NCV)

Love is the centre of our confidence—being loved by God and loving him and remaining in his love. Throughout our children's lives, they will continue to grow in knowing God's love and in loving him. They will also grow in using tools, skills and disciplines that enable them to remain in his love, to reposition themselves in God and to connect with him whenever they want.

My son began to struggle with being afraid in his room at night. We encouraged him to chat to God and he did, but he still wasn't really able to settle. We knew that the key was for him to meet with God about it, as 'perfect love drives out fear' (1 John 4:18). We were reminded of the verse 'Whatever is true, whatever is noble, whatever is right, whatever is pure, whatever is lovely, whatever is admirable—if anything is excellent or praiseworthy—think about such things' (Philippians 4:8), so I went and got a notebook, a pencil and a torch. My son couldn't write at the time, but he could draw, so I gave him the supplies and told him to draw pictures with God of all the wonderful things in his life—some beautiful thoughts, adventures he's gone on with God, and things and people he loves. I told him to draw lovely and excellent things with God until he fell asleep. He fell asleep easily that night. Even now, he keeps a pack filled with supplies in his bed because this is a tool he continues to use on his own when he is afraid at night.

As your children grow, think about gradually giving them tools to use that will enable them to express their love for God and to connect with his love in return so that they can 'remain in him' well.

Connect to community

- Hearts: Understand through curiosity; help children be powerful for the next time

Let's look again at those verses from John 15. After Jesus has encouraged us to remain in him, see what follows (highlighted in bold):

'I am the vine, and you are the branches. If any remain in me and I remain in them, they produce much fruit. But without me they can do nothing... I loved you as the Father loved me. Now remain in my love. I have obeyed my Father's commands, and I remain in his love. In the same way, if you obey my commands, you will remain in my love. I have told you these things so that you can have the same joy I have and so that your joy will be the fullest possible joy. **This is my command: Love each other as I have loved you. The greatest love a person can show is to die for his friends.'** (John 15:5, 9–13, NCV)

It appears that one of the other techniques for remaining in him and for existing in a world that hates us is to be rooted in a loving community, one that loves us and empowers us to love others. For some of us, this community is made up of good Christian friendships, but I would suggest that a church community can also challenge us to go deeper with God and equip us to live boldly in the world.

- Invest in your church; invest in those relationships. Invite people around for dinner when your children are awake so that they can participate in the conversations and play games with your friends. The more you can give them a multigenerational community of people who love God and love them, the more they will be able to live in a community of love, where people continually help them and encourage them to remain in God's love.

- Invest in your church; invest in those areas of service. Empower your children to join a ministry team and to serve on it faithfully and well. Release them to learn from others and to love God through service.
- Invest in your church; invest in learning. Help your children to engage with the service and the teaching. Encourage them to expect to be challenged and to grow deeper in their knowledge of God's word and in their encounter with him.

When your children are raised to invest in deep relationships with other Christians and with God himself, they will experience what Jesus promised—the fullest possible joy.

Ask your children curious questions to enable you to understand more of their experiences in church, with other Christian children and adults, at home and in their daily lives. The more you understand their hearts, the more you will be able to speak truth to their hearts and build a structure for relationships that will support them when they face the world. As they grow, they will begin to hold this value closely. When they leave our homes, their investment in relationships with God, his people and a church community will help them stay resilient against the world's pull.

*

— Chapter 11 —

Comparison and contentment

Key question: My children are constantly talking about how they want to be different, how they dislike bits of themselves and want to be like other people, to live like other people. How can I help my children to be content simply with who they are and where they are?

I think one of the moments that really tears at our hearts as parents is when we see our joyful, free children begin to shrivel and hide as they compare themselves with others and start to feel inadequate. When our children are pulled into comparisons, we often feel powerless to help because it has to do with what is going on inside them, and we feel locked outside.

The desire to compare is not new: 'I wish I were smarter/prettier/skinnier/taller/richer... If only I had [xxxx], then I could be happy.' With today's technology, our children aren't limited to comparing themselves with those in their immediate community; now they can compare themselves with people all around the world!

Comparison steals contentment because it pulls our children completely out of a God-centred core of confidence.

A God-centred core says this:

> God is awesome and holy, and he loves me totally and unreasonably.
>
> He is daily shaping me to be like him, and I am not finished yet.
>
> I am invited to be a small part of his wonderful plans.

But comparison breeds a core of confidence that says this:

> Some people are cool and competent and possess the right things, and they will be loved by all.
>
> If I can become one of them, I will be loved and I will have confidence in who I am.
>
> If I can prove to God that I'm worthy enough, maybe he will use me to do great things.

Comparison makes our children focus on themselves. It causes them to believe that their worthiness to be loved and be powerful rests in the eyes of others. They will always lose that battle: it will bring fear and isolation and will steal from them the blessing and peace of community and the belief that 'we are better together than we are apart'. Comparison robs our children of the joy of being loved by a powerful God.

A deeper look at the issue

Envy is one of the roots of comparison, one of the deep motivations that drive it. One definition of envy is 'the painful or resentful awareness of an advantage enjoyed by another joined with a desire to possess the same advantage' (www.merriam-webster.com/dictionary/envy).

God speaks a lot about envy in the Bible. Envy is even in one of the ten commandments: 'You shall not covet your neighbour's house. You shall not covet your neighbour's wife, or his male or female servant, his ox or donkey, or anything that belongs to your neighbour' (Exodus 20:17). One of Solomon's proverbs speaks to the centre of the matter: 'A heart at peace gives life to the body, but envy rots the bones' (Proverbs 14:30).

When we allow ourselves to look at other people and want what they have, be it material things, natural qualities, relationships or ways of life, we instantly begin the destructive cycle of comparison. When we allow ourselves to say, 'What they have is better than what I have', we also begin to think, 'Who they are is better than who I am.'

I don't think desire is unhealthy. We all have needs and hopes and desires. Scripture makes it clear that we are to bring them directly to God and lay them before him with trust and love. Envy develops when we take those desires and focus our attention on what we think the solution should be. 'I desire a job where I am making an impact' can quickly become 'I want *his* job. If I could only have that job, I would be happy.' Our children are no different. 'I desire good friends' can quickly become 'I want shoes and clothes and toys like hers. I want to be like her so that people will like me.' God's design is not for us to chase after wants, but for us to live in contentment and peace.

We often think that the path to contentment and peace is about creating a life with no wants, where there is enough of everything—but that is not true. Look at Paul. He was in prison in Rome when he wrote to his friends in Philippi:

I am not saying this because I am in need, for I have learned to be content whatever the circumstances. I know what it is to be in need, and I know what it is to have plenty. I have learned the secret of being content in any and every situation, whether well fed or hungry, whether living in plenty or in want. I can do all this through him who gives me strength. (Philippians 4:11–13)

Paul had managed to find a way to be content in circumstances that were incomplete and scary. Scripture repeatedly tells us that the key to peace is to have a grateful heart, being humbly conscious of who God is and what he has done (see Philippians 4:6–7). Contentment, at its core, is a combination of peace and gratitude in every situation.

The writer of Hebrews tells us:

Keep your lives free from the love of money and be content with what you have, because God has said, 'Never will I leave you;

never will I forsake you.' So we say with confidence, 'The Lord is my helper; I will not be afraid. What can mere mortals do to me?' (Hebrews 13:5–6)

I believe that contentment is inextricably linked to a God-centred core of confidence. So how do we raise our children to be content, positioned away from envy?

Putting the 'hearts and minds' tools into action

Here are a few suggestions to get you started in building a core of confidence.

Managing materialistic wants

- Hearts: Respond with empathy and truth
- Minds: Verbal framing; use foundational phrases

Our world bombards children with advertisements to feed their wants and desires. Our culture is constantly telling them, 'You need this. You need that. Look at what you don't have but really want!' When this happens, it instantly draws their eyes into a comparison: 'I have this, but I could have that. I am not content with what I have. I want more.' Envy seeps in.

Let's look at some of the main battlegrounds where we can help our children fight against envy.

Advertisements on television

In the UK we have several channels that don't show adverts, but many do. Adverts are designed specifically to push messages into your children's heads to make them feel discontented and envious. It's worth exposing this manipulation to your children so that they can see it for what it is. Have a chat about why adverts exist and how they are designed to make us want things. Highlight how ridiculous it is to think that owning a thing would make us happy, pretty, popular or cool. I would suggest that you regularly mute the adverts and, instead, use the time to talk or do other things. You can also watch programmes on a catch-up system so that you can fast-forward past the adverts. Picture a life at home with no adverts, with nothing speaking 'You need, you need…' into our children's heads.

Shopping with children

Walk into any supermarket or toyshop and you will join hundreds of other parents trying to wrestle with the 'But-I-really-want-you-to-buy-this-for-me-now' dance. Many families have found that having boundaries can be very helpful not just for managing behaviour but also for managing hearts. For instance, try offering your children as much choice as possible, so that they have some freedom in choosing cereal, types of apples or other everyday products. Also try setting a policy about heart attitude. In our family, saying, 'I want this', or 'I need this', or 'Please will you buy this for me' is off-limits. What we *can* say is, 'Oooo, look at this.

Isn't this interesting?' There is no expectation that anyone will purchase the thing that's been pointed out. We are just enjoying a trip and looking at interesting things along the way. I have, on occasion, made an impulse purchase for my family, but it was never in response to a demand, request or envious heart.

Gift giving and receiving

- Hearts: Understand through curiosity; help children be powerful for the next time
- Minds: Direct attention and values; equip children to be powerful in shaping their own minds

I have worked with many children and families over many years, and I have noticed that families with contented children tend to handle gift giving and receiving in similar ways. For most of us, gift giving is expected at birthdays and Christmas. Because gift givers want to ensure they are giving efficiently, they ask the person what they would like (or ask the parents what they think the child would like). Whether through the guise of writing letters to Santa or informing family and friends before a birthday or holiday, children are encouraged to ponder long and hard about what they want to receive. If they receive it, they are very happy. If they don't receive it, or if they receive something similar but not quite the same, then they might feel disappointed. In these cases, gratitude is dependent on receiving what they wanted.

The problem with this approach is that it deliberately

encourages children to envy, to look around and think, 'What do I want? What do I want you to get for me?' When that happens, they judge the gift giver according to whether he gave a 'good gift' or a 'bad gift'—whether the request was filled correctly or incorrectly. It also creates a culture of expectation—the idea that they deserve a gift because it is their birthday or because it is Christmas. The expectation removes the joy of the unexpected and not-demanded gift, and replaces it with a focus on the fulfilment of children's wants through relational obligations.

So what do we do? Every year our children go on a cycle of desiring things and expecting their desires to be met. I would suggest that we need to re-examine the way we do gift giving.

What would it look like if no one were allowed to ask for anything? What if birthdays were about celebrating the person, and gifts were a minor byproduct, or if Christmas was about cultivating our hearts towards blessing each other instead of focusing on what we were going to get?

I would suggest telling our children that gifts are just that—gifts. They are undeserved, unasked for, and come from the heart of the other person to you. They are not to be expected or hoped for, quantified or judged. A gift is about someone saying, 'I thought this might bring you joy.'

When we receive gifts, it is from a position of seeing the heart behind the gift. If Grandma gives you an old weird toy, it's because she loves you very much and she thought you might enjoy it. Be grateful that you have a grandma who loves you that much. Enjoy it! Teach your children to embrace what has been given instead of what could have been given. Raise children to pay attention to the hearts of the gift givers and to understand that gift giving is about relationship.

One day, when Jesus was watching people drop gifts into the temple treasury, he saw many rich people give extravagant 'good' gifts, but he also saw one poor woman give just two small coins, which were all she had. Jesus was touched and told his disciples that this woman 'gave more than all those rich people' (Mark 12:43, NCV). He saw the heart behind the gift—the sacrifice and the love that went into it. We can equip our children to look for that, too, so their eyes will not be on the 'good gifts' they desire but on the heartfelt relationships behind the gifts.

This also works the other way in gift giving. When we train our children to give gifts from their hearts, everything changes. Christmas provides the perfect opportunity to shift to giving gifts from the heart. You can coach your children through this by first asking questions:

- What does [xxx] love thinking about or playing with right now?
- What would make her laugh?
- What do you think he would love but hasn't seen yet?
- Is there anything she enjoys that would really help her in her work or with her hobbies?
- What gift expresses the way you feel about him?

When our children begin to understand that gifts are an expression of relationship, undeserved and not demanded, they can begin to access God's gifts with a greater freedom and a right heart as well. God gives us so many gifts—salvation, hope and comfort, to name a few. When our children have hearts of contentment, they can begin to be grateful for all the gifts God has freely given them, instead of being annoyed or disappointed when he hasn't given them exactly what they wanted. Learning how to live in gratitude for God's blessings and gifts is core to living free of comparison and envy. When children focus on who God is and the undeserved blessings and gifts they receive from him, their eyes won't be so focused on what people are demanding and receiving from others.

Deeper questions and heart connections

- Hearts: Understand through curiosity; respond with empathy and truth; connect children to God
- Minds: Equip children to be powerful in shaping their own minds

As we explore these ideas with our children, it is worth remembering that envy has deep roots within the heart. Envy and discontentment are not really about objects we want, but about the deeper roots of want and need. A great question to ask your children when they begin to react out of envy, wishing they were like someone else or wanting what others have, is this: 'How would your life be different if you had that thing? Why?'

As you ask deeper and deeper questions by following your curiosity, seek to understand what is going on in your child's heart. Affirm their feelings and bring in any truth you feel they need to understand. Share your journey. Empower them to take their needs and wants to God. Suggest that they tell God exactly what is on their heart, what they are thinking and feeling right now. They can do it in their head or out loud, but it's between them and God. Allow some quiet time for them and God to meet about it. Spend some time thanking God for who he is and how he is faithful to meet our needs, even our deep ones. When we do this, then something great comes—God's peace.

Do not worry about anything, but pray and ask God for everything you need, always giving thanks. And God's peace, which is so great we cannot understand it, will keep your hearts and minds in Christ Jesus. (Philippians 4:6–7, NCV)

As we encourage our children to engage with God, it is also essential that we help them to look for his provision, his movement, and his shaping in their lives. God is an active God, living and speaking and working among his people. After our children have brought their desires to God and his peace has come, we must also shape their hearts to expect him to be moving in response. Chat about how you can enable your eyes to stay on God, trusting in his plans and purposes.

Create some next steps to help your children combat envy in the future. Help them to make plans for the next time they feel envious of a friend in school, or embarrassed on the playground. They can quote scripture to themselves, sing a song, take themselves for a walk or write in their notebook. Help them to create their own plan to disciple their hearts in difficult circumstances.

*

— Chapter 12 —

Manliness and beauty

Key question: My son is really self-conscious
about being one of the smallest boys in his class,
and he keeps asking about how to get muscles.
I caught my daughter looking in the mirror,
and she asked me if she was fat. I feel as if I'm
watching my children really struggle with how
they look, and I'm getting worried. How do I help
my children negotiate the storm of images that
tell them what boys and girls are supposed to
look like?

Throughout history, cultures have defined what the ideal male and female forms look like. With the rise of multimedia outlets, we are experiencing an unprecedented level of communication targeted at us and our children, insisting that there is a deep value attached to what our bodies look like. They display ideal beauty or manliness and tell us what we should do in order to achieve it.

Fad diets, plastic surgery, corrective undergarments, fancy creams, dressing right for your shape, gym memberships and magazine articles all promise ways to correct our naturally unacceptable bodies into something that people will admire. Our children are growing up to be deeply dissatisfied with what they see in the mirror, and they are slowly getting sucked into a desire to pursue this ethereal, ultimate goal of beauty or manliness. They begin to judge themselves and they expect to be judged by others. At a younger and younger age, they become self-conscious and self-judging, wishing to be like someone else. It is affecting not only their confidence but also their participation in opportunities. A government study from 2012 showed that a significant majority of teenage girls who don't participate in activities like after-school clubs and sports choose to avoid them because of anxiety over their body image.[4] Eating disorders are increasing among children and teenagers of both genders, and we as parents are doing everything we can to try to bolster our children's confidence enough to stem the tide of negative messages.

There are excellent resources online and in books to help our children to be media literate and to understand the media's messages that stream towards them. But what does this topic look like from a spiritual point of view? If we are parenting our children with a biblical core of confidence, how does it help our sons and daughters in this world of physical obsession?

A deeper look at the issue

Beauty

At the very core of the body image issue, I believe, is the fact that the debate robs our children of their fullness. The primacy attached to an ideal body tells our children that their character, their heart, their mind, their passions, dreams, skills and giftings are all secondary to what is really important—the way they look. Beauty becomes the key to everything, from friends and romance to joy and confidence. It's not just about how they look; it's about what their physical appearance opens up for them—love, acceptance, praise and approval.

The reason why body image is a major battleground is that it forces children's eyes, hearts and minds to focus on the way they look and how they feel about the way they look. Body image demands that our children place themselves firmly at the centre of their confidence. This is why the issue is problematic for them.

On one side, the media and society bombard our children with images and values about what they should look like and feel like. Children are told that beauty (both male and female) looks like *this* and makes you feel powerful, free, fun, confident and irresistibly attractive.

The other side rises up and says, 'Yes, beauty *does* make you feel powerful, free, fun, confident and irresistibly attractive. But how dare you tell me it can only look like *that*! It can look like *this* too! Everyone is beautiful, and it is important that everybody knows it and believes it, so that they can feel all those things too.'

Both sides of the debate accept that 'beauty' is the key for all of us. They just disagree on what is classified as beautiful. We are encouraged to love ourselves and love our bodies, and we are told to believe that we are all truly beautiful so that we can all experience the rush of feeling powerful, free, fun, confident and irresistibly attractive.

The problem is that none of that reflects the Bible's view of beauty. Interestingly, beauty doesn't rank as anything important to God. The idea that our bodies are beautiful 'just the way we are', no matter what their shape, simply isn't in the Bible. God doesn't want our eyes focused on beauty. In fact, God tends towards the opposite. If he is enabling us to grow more like him, then our view of human beauty is to be the same as his:

Charm is deceptive, and beauty is fleeting; but a woman who fears the Lord is to be praised. Honour her for all that her hands have done, and let her works bring her praise at the city gate. (Proverbs 31:30–31)

But the Lord said to Samuel, 'Do not consider his appearance or his height, for I have rejected him. The Lord does not look at the things people look at. People look at the outward appearance, but the Lord looks at the heart.' (1 Samuel 16:7)

Your beauty should not come from outward adornment, such as elaborate hairstyles and the wearing of gold jewellery or fine clothes. Rather, it should be that of your inner self, the unfading beauty of a gentle and quiet spirit, which is of great worth in God's sight. (1 Peter 3:3–4)

In scripture, it appears that considering our own physical beauty isn't part of God's plan for our lives. What is important is the development of our hearts and minds, the inner beauty of a transformed life. That's not to say we are to deny any physical beauty that people ascribe to us, or to think ourselves ugly. Our job is not to convince ourselves that we are *not* beautiful according to the world's standards.

It is just that we are called to value other things far above worldly beauty, and to let our hearts and minds draw strength and confidence from those things. Remember our core of confidence:

> God is awesome and holy, and he loves me totally and unreasonably.
>
> He is daily shaping me to be like him, and I am not finished yet.
>
> I am invited to be a small part of his wonderful plans.

Personally, I know I am not beautiful according to the current standards. I don't say that to many people as they tend to get concerned that something is seriously wrong with my self-esteem and confidence, so they kindly try to rush in and assure me of my natural and unique beauty. The truth is, though, I don't seek or want to be beautiful by the world's standards. I don't worry about wrinkles or fat or what is in style or how my body looks. I want to pursue holiness and goodness and health; I want to love God fully, love others sacrificially and enjoy my friends and family and the world. I would much rather that people found me funny, loving, engaging, powerful and encouraging than that they found me beautiful. For someone to stop and praise the outside of me seems odd. It's as if someone was given a gift and spent most of her time focusing on the wrapping paper. The gift isn't about the wrapping! It's about what's inside. Our children are gifts to us and others, deep and multifaceted. Let's not allow them to think they are all about their wrapping.

When we as parents accept that beauty is valuable, we unwittingly make it a focus for our children. For both our boys and our girls, we need to shift our focus away from physical appearance and instead concentrate on their character and passions, because those are the issues on God's heart, and those are what will last an eternity.

This book has already explored some of the skills that will help us go on this journey with our children. Let's see how a few of them can apply specifically to this issue.

In Chapter 5 we talked about conversations that open up our children's hearts, to enable us to find the root of what is growing in them. We need to explore what the key of beauty would unlock. For instance, we could start by asking these questions. 'You said that you would love to look like [xxxx]. Why? What would change if you looked like him/her?'

In Chapter 6 we discussed the power of transforming our minds. One of the tools for shaping minds is to frame verbally what our children are seeing. My dad often stuck Post-It notes on my mirror and door, filled with little messages like these. 'I'm so proud of your bravery. I love seeing how hard you work—keep going! You are so precious to me. I'm so grateful you are my daughter.' I used to keep them on my mirror so that, as I got ready in the morning, I would be reminded of how my dad saw me. I learned to see that person in the mirror.

In Chapter 6 we also discussed the tool of directing our

children's attention to things. Explore how you describe other people. Do you comment on their appearance at all, or just the content of their character? How do you talk about yourself in front of your children? Consider having bold conversations with your children in which you tell them that you might have been focusing on the wrong thing, and invite them to see a little window into your journey of transforming your core of confidence.

In Chapter 8 we discussed how we can affirm our children within relationships instead of by using labels. In Chapter 9 we looked at how we can move away from labelling our children to praising the character traits we want to see growing in them. Have a think. What would it look like if you took the words 'beauty/beautiful' or 'handsome/manly' out of your vocabulary? How would you affirm your child? What godly traits in your children shine out of them from their core?

In a similar vein, when you greet children outside your family, how do you normally say hello? Often we comment on their outward appearance: 'My, what a beautiful coat!' 'You are looking fantastic today!' 'Don't you look nice?' 'What a beautiful baby!' 'Look at those muscles. What a strong little man!' 'He's just perfect!' Take time to ponder some new phrases to use and new questions to ask. Consider these: 'Good to see you! What book are you reading nowadays?' 'Well, hello, your face tells me you are happy today. What's made today so good?' 'My goodness, you were so kind when you helped your mummy open the door.'

Have a look back at Chapters 10 and 11, on media, and ponder specifically how your children engage with the messages of the media. What education do you need to give your children about how the media lie to us about beauty? Can you play 'Spot the lie' with advertisements that tie beauty to happiness or fun or friendship?

Romance and the future

I was recently watching a television programme in which some of the dialogue between a mother and teenage daughter struck me:

Daughter: I want to be pretty.
Mother: You are pretty.
Daughter: You are my mum. You have to say that. I want to be pretty to other people.

As our children grow, it is helpful to notice that, in our society, messages about beauty and attractiveness are linked to the possibilities of romance and future relational happiness. Sometimes the motivation behind our children's desire to embrace the beauty ideal is that they see it as the main way to finding future happiness in relationships. Think about all the movies, music, television programmes and books that communicate this message to our children. The idea of 'love at first sight' is a prevalent one, in which there's a beautiful woman who meets a devastatingly handsome and musclebound man, and instantly they're physically attracted to each other.

Children watch these storylines over and over again, and then they crave to be seen as beautiful or handsome because they want what that beauty will bring them—an instant admirer who sees them as worthy straight away and chooses them above all others. As they enter the preteen and teen years, children become focused on how they rank in attractiveness, and they want to learn how to become more beautiful or attractive. They can get involved in bad relationships because what they are seeking, based on the stories and messages they have been taught, is a partner who chooses them initially for their looks. They learn to seek out someone who will respond to the shallow value of beauty.

In order for our children to put aside this central value of beauty, they may need a broadening of the romance story they've been told. Most couple's love stories don't begin with 'I saw her across the room; I was overwhelmed by physical attraction, and I knew I wanted to marry her.' Most love stories are sweet and long and involve a slow-growing understanding of each other's character. Our children need to hear these stories. I would suggest that you invite friends around and invite them to tell their romance stories. Look for movies and books that tell the story of real love, deep love. Watch anniversary videos of elderly couples on YouTube, and read about disabled people who have found deep and powerful love.[5] Highlight stories about how God brings people together, so that children can continue to grow in their trust and hope in the Lord as he weaves their futures. May our children fully embrace a core of confidence that will bear much fruit in their lives.

*

Chapter 13

Comparison and humility

Key questions: God tells us that we are to be
humble. Are we really supposed to encourage
our children to think that other people are better
than them? Won't they get trampled on? Or
are we supposed to know how wonderful we
are and then choose to treat other people as if
they are better than us, even though we know
they're not? Isn't it damaging for our children to
go around thinking that other people are better
than them?

When we talk about confidence, often the question of humility comes up. Many people find the balance hard to achieve. We are familiar with scripture verses that say 'In humility value others above yourselves' (Philippians 2:3) and that we are to 'take the lowest place' (Luke 14:10). Our conclusions fuel some big questions for us about how we are to raise confident children who are also humble.

I believe that we have a warped view of what scripture means by humility. Our idea of humility becomes damaging when we allow the world to infect the idea. The world says that hierarchies are important. Who is the best, the one on top? Who is the worst? Who is worthy and who isn't? Sometimes, when we hear the word 'humility', we think we need to enter into those judgements about hierarchy, putting ourselves at the bottom, thinking that everyone else is better than us and considering ourselves less important than others. We can begin to believe that humility is about comparing ourselves with others and judging ourselves to be not as good. Rightly, something in us chafes against that idea, particularly when it comes to teaching it to our children.

The humility that we are called into by God has nothing to do with hierarchy, nothing to do with being 'better' or 'less' than others. It has nothing to do with comparisons. It has to do with two things—understanding who we are to God and understanding who we are to others.

A deeper look at the issue

Scripture tells us often that God wants us to be humble before him.

What does the Lord require of you? To act justly and to love mercy and to walk humbly with your God. (Micah 6:8)

Humble yourselves, therefore, under God's mighty hand, that he may lift you up in due time. (1 Peter 5:6)

For the Lord takes delight in his people; he crowns the humble with victory. (Psalm 149:4)

Humbling ourselves before God means simply living out the first sentence of our core of confidence: 'God is awesome and holy, and he loves me totally and undeservedly.' It means understanding who God is and who we are, imperfect and small in the face of such a mighty and wonderful God. When we enable our children to understand that 'it's not about me but about him', then their hearts can have the right sort of humility—seeing their own fragility and smallness compared with a mighty, powerful and loving God—and they can have the joy of being loved by him.

Most of us, as parents, feel comfortable with this aspect of humility. It feels right. What causes us more concern, though, is the way in which our children are called to walk humbly with their peers. It's easy to know that we are nothing compared with God, but what if we are comparing ourselves with other people?

As we have seen, true humility isn't about hierarchy. It isn't about thinking that we are rubbish and others are much better than us. It isn't about comparison or competition. It's simply about loving and serving others well. It's about making others a priority in our decision-making processes. It's about delighting in being a small part of a community that, together, is a greater representation of the essence of Jesus than we are as individuals, apart from each other.

I have already mentioned the need to 'value others above yourselves', but look at this verse in its context. Paul was writing to a new church and encouraging its members to live like Jesus, loving each other in unity and service:

Therefore if you have any encouragement from being united with Christ, if any comfort from his love, if any common sharing in the Spirit, if any tenderness and compassion, then make my joy complete by being like-minded, having the same love, being one in spirit and of one mind. Do nothing out of selfish ambition or vain conceit. Rather, in humility value others above yourselves, not looking to your own interests but each of you to the interests of the others. (Philippians 2:1–4)

When Paul says, 'Value others above yourselves', he is talking about where we allow our hearts to rest, and how we make decisions. For Paul, humility is about removing selfishness as the main force behind our decisions and, instead, putting our desire to love, serve and lift up others as the main force. It isn't about tearing ourselves down, a process of making ourselves feel inadequate or 'less than' others. It's about repositioning our hearts. Humility is a way of feeling and thinking that insists on love and service to God and others staying central, so that we can truly 'love the Lord your God with all your heart and with all your soul and with all your mind' and 'love your neighbour as yourself' (Matthew 22:37, 39).

How do we parent for this outcome? How do we empower our children to walk confidently with strength and humility, without giving in to the world's view of comparison and hierarchy?

Putting the 'hearts and minds' tools into action

Here are a few suggestions to get you started in building a core of confidence.

Seeing others and judging

- Minds: All tools

We start with shaping the way our children perceive other people when they see and encounter them. The way our culture is set up, it is easy to see others as rivals in the competition of life—rivals for friends, for status and for success.

As Christians, though, we are called simply to see others as people whom God loves and sacrificed himself for. We are called to see people who are loved by God, who aren't finished yet but are still a small part of his wonderful plans. Some are far from him and haven't met him yet; some are connected to him and are on their journey to becoming more like him; but all are loved by him, with God-designed plans and purposes for their life. Our role is to be humble, and serve and love.

I believe that this is why Jesus was so outspoken about judging others. I love the way Jesus explains it here:

'Do not judge, or you too will be judged. For in the same way as you judge others, you will be judged, and with the measure you use, it will be measured to you. Why do you look at the speck of sawdust in your brother's eye and pay no attention to the plank in your own eye? How can you say to your brother, "Let me take the speck out of your eye," when all the time there is a plank in your own eye? You hypocrite, first take the plank out of your own eye, and then you will see clearly to remove the speck from your brother's eye.' (Matthew 7:1–5)

Let's look closer at these verses. First of all, Jesus indicates that my sin, my faults and weaknesses, my incompleteness, can be greater than the other person's and yet I can still see their faults as the primary problem. So often, our children spot the wrongs in others and yet feel totally justified in their own experience of sin and wrong choices. As we parent for confidence, it is helpful to train our children to reflect more on what God is doing in them than on what God is doing in others. When a conflict arises, children may want to blame others and discuss the wrongness of others. They may want to gossip about others' failings and rejoice in others' downfalls. This contributes to their desire to be better than others, to see others' weaknesses and faults as larger than their own—and, as a consequence, they can feel superior to others.

As these moments arise, take time to reinforce the idea that everyone is on a journey and no one is perfect yet. Discuss the children's experience of the event or issue, and coach them through what is going on in their own hearts and minds. It is not their place to judge other people, but, instead, to grow as much as they can on their own journey in each circumstance.

The second thing that strikes me is in the first two verses: 'Do not judge, or you too will be judged. For in the same way as you judge others, you will be judged, and with the measure you use, it will be measured to you.' I believe this is a really poignant truth. The way our family judges other people is the way our children will learn to judge others, and, through that, they learn how to judge themselves. Judging others is often a part of everyday conversation.

'Did you see what she was wearing? I just don't get it.'

'Whoa, look how much weight he's lost. He looks amazing!'

'I was so bored talking to Joe. Why didn't you rescue me? He is so annoying.'

'Did you hear about John's new job? He just keeps getting promoted.'

From the way other people structure their family life to what they eat and where they go, little judgements can seep into everyday life. We even train our children how to judge us as their parents: 'Ugh, I'm so lazy today' or 'I'm so hopeless with bills.' Quickly we can create a life pattern for children that encourages their natural sinful propensity to judge others according to the world's standards. Then they begin to get a hardened heart towards others, and they begin to feel superior. Ultimately, their compassion lessens.

When we judge, our sinful desire to be better than someone else emerges. Our broken world sets up standards for us to achieve and then celebrates or ridicules us, according to how well we have achieved those standards. Whether it's about success at school, a high-paying job, a good standard of living, a popular personality, or the way we look and behave, we are all surrounded with 'ideals' to achieve, and how we are doing at achieving those ideals becomes a competition. Who is better? Who can be the best?

What is also scary is that our children take all of those judgement criteria and apply them to themselves. When we look at other people and call them fat, and then we look at ourselves and complain about our bodies, we have communicated effectively to our children that their bodies are supposed to look a certain way and that people will judge them if their bodies aren't perfect. When we comment on other people's jobs or successes or failures, children learn that they should be judged by that measure, too.

The way we train our children to see others is the way they will see themselves. The way we train our children to see *us* is the way they will see themselves.

Think about these questions. What do you say about others when you are watching television or walking down the road? How do you speak about the people at church on your way home or about your colleagues and friends? How do you speak about yourself? What judgements are you encouraging in your family, and what are you training your children to see in you?

Now ponder these. How do we *want* our children to see others? How do we want them to see themselves?

Scripture says that we are not to compare ourselves with other people or to judge others. Our measuring stick is Jesus (Ephesians 4:13). We know that 'everyone has sinned and fallen short of God's glorious standard' (Romans 3:23, NCV), so we simply walk the path of knowing the core of confidence in our own lives:

God is awesome and holy, and he loves me totally and unreasonably.

He is daily shaping me to be like him, and I am not finished yet.

I am invited to be a small part of his wonderful plans.

We are also called to believe the same of other people. We are called to believe that God loves *them* totally and unreasonably; he is daily shaping *them* to be like him, and *they* are not finished yet; but *they* are still invited to be a small part of his wonderful plans on earth. It isn't our place to judge them for where they are on their journey with God. What we can do, instead, is to expect to see God at work in each person's life.

When our children have this viewpoint, they can begin to look for the good in others instead of the sin and incompleteness. They can see each person as loved and valuable, knowing that God is growing and being refined in each one.

Think back to Chapter 9, where we talked about praising what we want to see growing in our children. We discussed considering all the biblical character traits that God is developing in our children and how we could encourage our children within that context. I would suggest that the list you use to encourage your children can also be used when you discuss others. When you tell stories from work or see people you know at church or notice random people on the street, what are you going to draw your children's attention to? Try noticing others' perseverance, love or connection with God. Invite your children to tell stories of their friends, highlighting their good points. When you leave someone's house, ask each family member these questions: 'What did you really like about them? How did we see them being a bit like God?' Discuss how you learn about God through other people, or how you are challenged by their circumstances and how they are coping.

In speaking about others, what would it look like if we

as families truly considered living by Paul's encouragement in Ephesians?

Do not let any unwholesome talk come out of your mouths, but only what is helpful for building others up according to their needs, that it may benefit those who listen. And do not grieve the Holy Spirit of God, with whom you were sealed for the day of redemption. Get rid of all bitterness, rage and anger, brawling and slander, along with every form of malice. Be kind and compassionate to one another, forgiving each other, just as in Christ God forgave you. (Ephesians 4:29–32)

When we do this, our children will begin to see others as loved, imperfect people whom we can value and learn from, and they can consider themselves to be the same.

Not designed to be alone

• Minds: All tools

One of the reasons that true humility is about loving and serving God and other people, as a central position of our heart, is that Christians are not designed to be alone. We are designed to be together as the body of Jesus Christ.

Do not think of yourself more highly than you ought, but rather think of yourself with sober judgment, in accordance with the faith God has distributed to each of you. For just as each of us has one body with many members, and these members do not all have the same function, so in Christ we, though many, form one body, and each member belongs to all the others. We have different gifts, according to the grace given to each of us. If your gift is prophesying, then prophesy in accordance with your faith; if it is serving, then serve; if it is teaching, then teach; if it is to encourage, then give encouragement; if it is giving, then give generously; if it is to lead, do it diligently; if it is to show mercy, do it cheerfully.

Love must be sincere. Hate what is evil; cling to what is good. Be devoted to one another in love. Honour one another above yourselves. Never be lacking in zeal, but keep your spiritual fervour, serving the Lord. Be joyful in hope, patient in affliction, faithful in prayer. Share with the Lord's people who are in need. Practise hospitality. (Romans 12:3–13)

As individuals, we were never designed to be the whole package. We weren't made to be the best at everything, comprehensively better than other people. We were deliberately shaped to be puzzle pieces, incomplete in and of ourselves, but fitting together as the body of Christ. If we train our children to think that life is about a hierarchy, we are robbing them of the delight of being a part of the body of Christ. When they see themselves as pieces of God's great plan, they are not surprised or hurt by others, and they are not competitive with them; they genuinely delight in and are grateful for people who are shaped differently from them.

When we teach our children that together we are stronger than when we are apart, and that having weaknesses is not only OK but necessary, then they can relax. When the stress of having to be it all and do it all goes away, all that is left is to trust our magnificent God to guide us, and to be faithful in playing our parts as he asks us to. As small parts of his body and his big plan, we can trust that God is weaving things together for good, and we can develop a deep sense of value in working as a team.

Here are a few suggestions for how we can begin to develop this value with our children. (If you want to find out more, *Parenting Children for a Life of Purpose* explores the concept in full.)

Make sure your child knows that God is active and doing things in the world, and that he invites us, individually and together, to follow him and see lives and communities transformed. Talk about what God is doing in the world and what his activity looks like. When you read the Bible with your children, highlight God's plans and purposes for people's lives and for their towns and cities, and highlight the way God worked with people to bring about wonderful change and to put his love and himself at the centre again. Jesus said that he only did what he saw the Father doing (John 5:19). Help your children to understand what the Father is doing and to know how you, in particular, have learned to do what he is doing.

Watch movies, YouTube or Upworthy clips about what God is doing around the world in and through people. Note that the stories often focus on one individual as the 'hero', but that the individual actually has many people around him or her, with different skills and personalities, who together form a great team.

For example, South Korean pastor Lee Jong-rak saw a desperate need in his community: women were abandoning their babies on the streets. When he felt God's heart for these little ones, God raised up a team around him. They made a box in which women could place their babies safely; when the women did so, Lee Jong-rak and others committed themselves to raising these children by opening an orphanage. Today they are raising children in South Korea to know that they are loved by God and others. The project needed teams of all kinds, from people who loved cooking to those who loved rocking babies, to those who could handle the politics and paperwork to get money and attention. Teams of all ages and shapes and sizes were needed, and together they continue to save children's lives.

Watch videos that focus on one person, and point out the helpers in the background, the teams around the individual. Highlight the fact that one person can never achieve as much as the team together.

Train your children to take genuine delight in other people and their accomplishments. Talk about what is wonderful about everyone you meet, even the difficult people. Share your stories of how you choose to look at the good things in people, instead of focusing on the bad. Model how to think through the different skills and gifts you need on your team for a project, and brainstorm together who would be perfect to invite into the team with you. Ask your children questions and help them process how to genuinely love and serve other people. Ask regularly, 'What can we do to help lift this person up, so that others can see those great things about them?'

Create a deep value for teamwork within your family. Build foundational phrases that encourage teamwork: 'Go, Team Turner. Let's team it! We are much more powerful together. Let's make it happen as a team!' Reward team thinking. Create challenges that your children can complete only if they work together. Praise creative thinking and the use of each other's skills and gifts. Praise children for submitting to each other's strengths and delighting in them, instead of fighting about who can do things best. The more our children learn to think as a team and to prefer teams, the more comfortable they will feel in not having to do everything alone.

Developing a healthy view of competition

- Hearts: All tools
- Minds: Direct attention and values

When we begin to look at humility, we might wonder about the nature of competition. Some of our children are naturally competitive, and the way this quality plays out in their lives is an important question.

There are many aspects of competition—personal, professional, relational, and formal competition in terms of sports and the like. I find it helpful to consider the heart behind it all. As we discussed at the beginning of this chapter, the world categorises people according to success, according to who is best. We have award shows for theatre, movies and sporting competitions. We have popular music chart winners, restaurant stars and online rankings of the most popular or attractive people. The world ingrains in our children, at a very early age, that being the best at something is essential to happiness and success. So, at its worst, a drive to be competitive is a symptom of the desire to be better than others, to succeed and feel proud of oneself for being the best. It's about comparing ourselves with others and proving ourselves to be at the top. If this is at the core of what drives our children, it will always be damaging to their integrity and their heart.

There is a way, though, of humbly engaging with competition without being competitive. It just takes a heart shift—a different path of progression.

If we can channel our children into keeping their eyes on themselves instead of on others, then competition takes on a new aspect. If we train them to have a heart that says, 'I am not finished yet, and God is daily shaping me to be more like him', then we can empower them to embrace and work in partnership with the journey of personal transformation. What if competitiveness wasn't about being better than someone else, but about an internal drive for excellence? What if it was about wanting to be better tomorrow than we were today—achieving more, improving more and pushing our bodies and minds to greater and greater possibilities? What if it was about giving our best, in heart, soul and mind?

A heart of humility in competition delights in challenge and also delights in competitors. A sportsman can be a shining light of God's love, generosity and service while he is still competing. What happens in our hearts defines a right or wrong engagement with competition.

It's about the difference between saying, 'I want to be the best actor/singer/tennis player/leader in the world and crush my opponents' and saying, 'I want to be the best actor/singer/tennis player/leader that I can be, and serve others in love and humility while I try.' As parents, we are called to disciple our child's character as they develop their ambitions. So yes, let's encourage and empower our children to pursue excellence; let's release our children into the activities that they passionately want to pursue; but let's also remember to disciple their hearts and minds while they do it.

Use curious questions to monitor children's motivations. When you see children becoming stressed or overcompetitive in a negative way, begin to open up conversations using the tools from Chapter 5 ('Hearts'). Help them uncover what is going on in their root system that is causing the stress, and minister into it. This approach applies to all types of competition, from students' test results to children's video games. Say, 'You seemed so [xxxx]. Why were you feeling that? What do you wish had gone differently? How did you want it to go? Which part did you enjoy? If I could give you a magic clock to erase one minute, which minute would it be?'

Playing games gives us plenty of opportunities to equip children with healthy views of competition. When you play games at home, set some boundaries around attitude as well as behaviour. For instance, what sort of language do you allow, and what body language? I would suggest that much gloating and superiority can be seen during game playing at home, from board games to football, which trains our children's beliefs about what is acceptable in competition. Have a look at the way children treat each other while playing a board game, and how some adults gloat over being the best, and you will see much in common between them. Do we allow gloating or celebrating others' failures or faults? Do we laugh at each other's mistakes? Do we allow each other to call people 'loser' or to celebrate a win too enthusiastically?

Or do we insist on encouraging and generous attitudes while playing, so that everyone feels valued?

I'm not saying that children should not play to win, because I think we should allow them to push themselves to excellence in all areas of their lives, but we need to disciple them to do it generously and with consideration for others. They can strive for their best, but they should not strive to be better than others.

Invite to your house Christians who excel in the fields your children are interested in, and who walk humbly and well in their professions. Ask them questions about integrity and competition. Invite them to tell stories of their journey and how they manage to serve and love others while also pursuing their best with all their strength.

Enable your children to describe themselves in terms of their passions and character, not according to what they are best at. We often describe children by picking out one or two main characteristics, to make it easier to talk about them, and we base our description on what they are best at, compared with the other children. For example, we might say, 'This is Alice, and she's our intellectual. This is George. He's our sporty one. This is Katherine, our drama queen extraordinaire.' These labels can cause our children to make connections between their personal identity and the things they are better at doing than others. This is part of the reason we see children being mean to each other or trying to prevent others from improving their own abilities. If a child's identity is wrapped up in an attitude of superiority, seeing anyone else's success causes fear, hurt and instability. Instead, try saying something like, 'This is Alice, our oldest.

Alice, what have you been really interested in investigating lately? This is George. He has recently taken up leading his team and is doing a great job of ensuring that all members feel really valued. And this is Katherine. Whenever she is with us, she brings us great joy.'

Our tendency to describe children according to what they can do better than others also prevents them from embracing the fact they are multifaceted and ever changing. It is OK for a child to love the flute, even though his sister loves it too and is better at playing it. If the flute brings him joy, he should keep playing the flute. It is all right to be a mediocre football player if the sport brings joy. A child might be sporty and dramatic today, and tomorrow the same child might decide she loves science and maths. It doesn't matter if your children are the best at any of it, because God is awesome and holy, and he loves them totally and unreasonably. He is daily shaping them to be like him, and they are not finished yet. They are invited to be a small part of his wonderful plans.

We need to be careful how we encourage our children when they are struggling over comparisons with others. Our language can accidentally set up a hierarchy in their minds. I have heard many parents say to their children, 'The others are just jealous, and that's why they are mean to you.' Parents often say this because they want their children to believe that because they are so clearly better than others, people are unable to handle their own envy. The children then distance themselves from anyone mean or hostile because of their condescending belief that they truly are better than the others, which perpetuates the tension. Some parents will go further and encourage their children to rise above and be 'the better person' or 'the bigger person'. This language isn't helpful either; in fact, it could make the problem even worse.

When our children learn to walk with confidence in humility, they will make themselves available to be used by God in significant ways. As we read through the Bible, we see over and over again that humility was a key character trait in those who were strong in the faith—Moses, Joseph, Job, Deborah, David, Paul, Barnabas and, ultimately, the greatest of them all, Jesus. We have excellent examples before us.

*

— Chapter 14 —

Failure

Key question: My child gets really upset when he loses or fails at something. It really knocks his confidence, and I have a hard time getting him to want to try again. How can I help him be confident even through failure?

Failure is the true test of our children's core of confidence. If their confidence is centred on themselves, then, when they are excelling or succeeding, it will be flying high. But when they fail or don't achieve what they set out to achieve, their confidence crumbles, and building it back up again can be a long process. Failure can feel like a real threat to children, and often they treat it as something to be fearfully avoided at all costs.

A deeper look at the issue

In order to help our children engage effectively with failure instead of fearing it, we ourselves need a healthy view of failure. Let's take a look at a few pointers.

First, failure is natural. Children will have been dealing with failure since they were born, whether reaching for toys, crawling, walking, or tying their shoelaces. Their lives have been full of things they wanted to do but couldn't do yet.

Failure is a natural part of the growing process, familiar in everyday life. At some point in their lives, though, our children begin to become self-conscious about failing. This change happens not naturally but culturally, as a result of being in a world that values success and perfection.

Second, failure is strategic. We often become frustrated when we're confronted with the possibility of failure, and with failure itself when it happens, but this is a refining process through which God is able to work in our lives and develop us in specific areas. Remember when the disciples were caught in a storm and Jesus calmed the sea (Mark 4:35–41). If we look back to the beginning of the story, we find that it was Jesus who suggested to the disciples that they should all cross over to the other side of the sea: he deliberately led them out to the place where the storm would develop. He created a situation in which the disciples could succeed or fail, and, in their moment of failure, he taught them valuable truths that laid the foundation for their future ministry.

Remember when the Israelites were brought to the edge of the promised land (Numbers 14). God gave them the opportunity to move into their new land, but they failed to choose bravely to follow him. God then led the Israelites into the desert for 40 years in order to build a generation that would trust in him, and, as a result, when he brought the people back to the edge of the promised land, they were ready to battle with boldness and confidence.

Paul writes in Romans 5:3–5:

We also glory in our sufferings, because we know that suffering produces perseverance; perseverance, character; and character, hope. And hope does not put us to shame, because God's love has been poured out into our hearts through the Holy Spirit, who has been given to us.'

Sometimes God leads us into places of difficulty to stretch us, teach us and empower us. It is here that we develop character and hope, which ultimately bring us back to God's love. To our eyes the situation can look like a complete failure, but God uses every failure as a wonderful training opportunity to equip us for the future he has called us to.

Third, failure is necessary. If we are going to enable our children to learn and grow, we must acknowledge that failure will be a key part of the learning process. After all, we can't learn something well without making some errors along the way. If our children are afraid of failure, they may hide from growing, learning or taking the risks that lead to great reward and greater maturity. If we truly want our children to have a core of confidence that says, 'God is awesome and holy, and he loves me totally and unreasonably. He is daily shaping me to be like him, and I am not finished yet. I am invited to be a small part of his wonderful plans,' they will have to accept that they are not finished yet. They are imperfect people who will make mistakes and will need to learn, often through trial and error.

When we, as parents, can see failure as a natural, strategic, necessary part of our imperfect children's everyday journey with God, then we can proactively build in them a framework through which they rightly experience current and future failure. We can help to shape failure as a process of life instead of as a crushing blow.

Putting the 'hearts and minds' tools into action

Here are a few suggestions to get you started in building a core of confidence.

Value effort, learning and progress over perfection

- Minds: Direct attention and values

Make effort, learning and progress key parts of what you praise and reward in your family. Acknowledge and celebrate how hard your children work, the determination and perseverance they show, and how wonderful their efforts are. Encourage them to see that it isn't about being *the* best; it's just about doing *their* best in a particular situation or set of circumstances. Help your children to see how far they have come and how much they have improved. Celebrate the improvement with much joy. Encourage them to teach you what they are learning, and be genuinely interested in the information. If you give rewards, consider rewards for concentration, positive attitude, perseverance and giving their best.

Celebrate character within the failure or success

- Heart: All tools
- Minds: Direct attention and values; verbal framing

When you talk with your children after their opportunities or events, celebrate the character they showed in the journey as much as, or even more than, you celebrate the success of the opportunity or event. Say, 'When you forgot your line, you could have let it distract you, but you handled it with such peace and grace, and you totally recovered and kept going. I wanted to cheer! That was well done, son. You fixed it so fast, I don't think anyone noticed' or, 'I loved watching you from the sidelines. You were so encouraging to every player when they went on or off the field. I could tell that you are a key part of that team. You really made a difference to your teammates.'

Take your children out to celebrate a catastrophic failure. Debrief them about the event and praise all the little successes that happened in the midst of it—goals they achieved mid-game, improvements they saw in their own performance, things they tried but that didn't work (or did). Rejoice in the fact that they tried something bold, no matter how it ended. Allow your children the space to process their emotions about the day. Ask questions so that you understand better how they feel and why: 'When that happened, what were you thinking? How did it make you feel? What made you choose this over that?' Affirm their feelings and help them find the truth in their moment of vulnerability.

Make experimentation a pattern of play and investigation

- Minds: Direct attention and values; equip children to be powerful in shaping their own minds

Experimentation is a learning tool, and too often we relegate it to the classroom. It's a great way to train our children to see failure as a strategic opportunity. When we remove experimentation from our homes and lives, our children see failure as only bad, as opposed to seeing it as a potentially helpful tool.

The easiest way to introduce experimentation is to create safe opportunities for our children to explore new ideas in parallel to what you are already doing. For instance, one day when I was making bread with my son, I deliberately made a double batch and asked him, 'What would happen if we put more yeast in?' His mischievous eyes widened and he said, 'Or *juice*?' So we split up the dough into three mounds and experimented with two of them. We tried juice in one and quadrupled the yeast in another. The results were not good, of course, but we learned a lot and had fun in the process.

Try asking 'What would happen if...?' questions, and then go about conducting the experiments. You might play games backwards or shrink old clothes that you were going to throw away, just to see if the process really works. Some of your experiments will have positive results, and some will be failures. After the experiments, review what happened and discuss what the children learned through the experience. Children can even strengthen their experimenting muscles by playing games that require perseverance and constant failure, like puzzles or Cluedo. By experimenting and learning from those experiences, children will grow in being able to handle failure better. When our children truly face difficult times in which they try something and fail, they will have a wealth of experiences to help them see their failures as learning points along a journey of growth.

Value growing in competence

- Hearts: Understand through curiosity; help children to be powerful for the next time

The second statement in the core of confidence is this: 'He is daily shaping me to be like him, and I am not finished yet.' This implies that today I am more shaped and capable than I was yesterday, and that the growth comes from acquiring competence. Competence is the ability to do something successfully. As we give our children opportunities to persevere and acquire competence, they will grow in the knowledge that if they can't conquer a task today, they can conquer it the next time. They can learn a new skill today and feel prepared to continue to the next challenge.

Caleb's brow was furrowed in frustration as he clutched the yogurt pot to his chest, one hand scraping across the top.

'How's it going, bud?' I asked.

With a grunt he replied, 'Hard. I can't do it.'

'Yes, you can. Try a new way!' I called out. He had been trying to get this lid off for about three minutes. Then I saw him start to squeeze the pot as hard as he could to pop the lid off. A part of my brain started screaming about the mess it would make, and everything in me just wanted to walk over, take the pot out of his hands, open it for him and hand it back. But I didn't. 'Interesting approach,' I murmured. I decided I would choose to let it happen. 'If it explodes everywhere,'

I thought, 'well, then he'll never try that again. Plus, we'll get to talk about pressure and why things explode, and he'll learn about the clean-up required. All positive things.'

After five minutes of struggling, he finally discovered the right angle at which to hold the pot. As he opened it, he cried out in triumph, 'I did it! I kept trying and I did it!'

I leaped off my chair and hooted with pride as well. 'Great persevering, Caleb! You didn't give up and you learned! Go you!'

He did a little dance and then proceeded to lick the lid. Once he'd settled down to eating, he debriefed me on what he'd learned and how he felt. He was so proud of himself. He was so chuffed with the result. His eyes gleamed with confidence.

Five minutes before, everything in me had wanted to rob my son of this moment of learning, just for a little personal convenience. I'm not saying we should never speed things along or offer help to our children, but a byproduct of enabling our children to be 'not finished yet' is that we empower them to trust in their ability to learn, to persevere, to improve, to solve their own problems and, ultimately, to grow in competence.

A family I know empowers all three of their children, aged five, seven and ten, to get themselves ready in the morning. The children wake themselves up at 7.00 am, and then they have an hour to eat, get dressed and be ready at the door by 8.00 am. At exactly 8.00 am, they walk out of the door in whatever state of readiness they have reached. If one decides to sleep in and miss breakfast, well, that's his choice. If another forgets to make sure she has clean socks ready to wear, it's her job to decide what to do. I chatted with the seven-year-old about it, and he told me, 'I'm using Post-it notes to remind myself of what to pack and bring to school in the morning, but it's not working very well. It only works some of the time. I'm going to try something new this week. I'm going to try to pack my bag the night before and see if that works better.' His occasional failures have resulted in many mishaps in the morning, but he laughed at them and sparkled with his plans to do better in the future. His ability to grow in competency at his own rate means that his failures are just learning tools instead of frustrations.

Clean up your mess and see God's redemption

- Minds: Direct attention and values; encounter God and his truth; equip children to be powerful in shaping their own minds

Often our children feel powerless when they fail or make a mistake, because they don't know what to do next. It can be helpful for them to know that they can clean up their messes, physically and emotionally. When we equip them to respond to their own mistakes, instead of swooping in to nag them and fix things for them, we can coach them to deal with failures in a proactive instead of a paralysing way. Whether they have spilt a drink or hurt a friend, we can expect them to clean up their messes, practically as well as relationally, and we can volunteer to help them think through their options.

Failure is not an end point. It isn't a full stop. It's one moment in the midst of a whole story, and what happens next is more important than the failure itself. When your child makes a mistake or fails, try asking them, 'What are you going to do? Do you need any ideas?' instead of rushing in to sort it out for them. Coach them in how to take the next steps toward fixing their failure. We can also encourage our children that 'in all things God works for the good of those who love him, who have been called according to his purpose' (Romans 8:28). As they are fixing whatever they can in the face of their mistake or failure, God is also working to pour his grace into the situation and will be working to bring good out of it as well.

Use stories of failure from your own life and from the Bible

- Hearts: Connect children to yourself and God
- Minds: Encounter God and his truth

As we have noted before, stories are powerful. Share some of your own everyday stories of failure. Tell your children how you think about those situations, how you felt and how you responded. Talk about what God did in response. Read Bible stories that focus on people's failures. So often, children only hear the stories of how our favourite biblical characters succeeded, but the very same people experienced massive failures as well. Share the stories of Peter denying Jesus, Paul failing to understand who Jesus was until he met him on the road to Damascus, Miriam grumbling against her brother Moses, Abraham lying about his wife, and David murdering Uzziah. They all failed miserably, but what did

God do? How did they clean up their messes? How did God work things out for good?

You can even watch secular movies and talk about failure. I find *Meet the Robinsons* a wonderful film for this topic. Why not have a movie night and discuss it as you watch?

Deal with self-criticism

- Hearts: All tools
- Minds: All tools

One major concern for parents arises when some of our children find themselves in a self-criticism loop. They can't forgive themselves for making a mistake, and we can feel powerless to help. Here are a few suggestions that might help when you feel that your children are beating themselves up about a situation.

Shame

Sometimes, children feel the burden of sin when they fail, and they don't know what to do with it. It is helpful to highlight the difference between a mistake and a sin. Many children carry shame about a mistake they have made, and we can give them the freedom to let it go.

Understand through curiosity: have a deep conversation to understand the root of their shame. To get you started, you might say, 'Sometimes when things happen, they sit on our heart, and we find it hard to stop thinking about them or thinking about our part in them. Have you ever felt that way?' or 'What do you wish was different about this situation right now?' Maybe they think they should be better or that people won't like them any more. They could be afraid or angry. Once you discover the root of their shame, you will be able to respond with empathy and truth, and you can help them create some next steps.

Connect them to God and others: God is the one who can deal with sin; he is the one who can restore lightness to our children. Sometimes they need to be reminded that when Jesus died on the cross and came back to life, he took upon himself all our sins and the punishment for all the things we have done wrong. It can be helpful to tell them that sometimes we want to punish ourselves for things we've done wrong, because we know they were wrong and we feel so bad about them, but Jesus died and rose again so that we don't have to carry those things with us.

If your child is up for it, pray with her. Tell God that she is holding on to things in her heart and that you are grateful to Jesus because he can take them away. Suggest to her that, in her mind, she can show God a picture of her heart and how it's feeling. Wait in silence as she does this. Then, suggest that whenever she is ready, she can ask Jesus to take away all the heaviness on her heart. Wait for a little bit more, and then thank God for his love and check in with your daughter about how she is feeling.

Self-labels

Children can come out with some scathing self-labelling. This is when we are most tempted to try the opposite labelling game. A child says, 'I'm rubbish,' and we want to rush in with 'No, you're not. You are amazing and perfect!' Instead of getting trapped into a label competition, try one of these strategies, depending on your child and the situation.

If you don't know where the label is coming from or what the situation was that kicked up that feeling, pursue understanding through curiosity, in conversation, until you understand what is going on. Then deal with it.

If your child is labelling himself out of frustration or anger, or he's unconsciously repeating things he's heard, try taking the direct approach of disciplining the lie. We normally don't allow blatant lies about other people to exist in our home. We wouldn't allow our child to bully his friend or sibling consistently with a label like 'rubbish', 'bad at everything' or 'useless', but we often allow children to believe lies about themselves. I tend to take each of these lies just as seriously, saying, 'You are not rubbish. That isn't the truth. We speak the truth in this family. What is the truth?' If your child struggles to find the truth, you can always help: 'The truth is that you are my son whom I love, who works hard and isn't finished growing in Maths yet, but you are getting better all the time', or, 'The truth is that God has a great purpose for you, regardless of what you think you are good at.'

Sometimes a more light-hearted approach can help. You can try playing a game using a lie jar. When one child catches another lying about himself (such as 'I have no friends'), the first one can call it out and tell the truth: 'That's not true. You have three friends who like you a lot, and all of us love you—ha!' The one who brings truth can get a reward from the jar, or the one voicing the lie needs to put something in: you decide. Also, you could write all the truths on Post-it notes and cover your child's door with them to remind him of the truth and to make him feel loved.

Failure is a wonderful and precious opportunity for growth, and we have the chance to walk our children through it. We can train them to cope with failure positively, so that they can live well in a world that sees failure as catastrophic and fear-filled. Our children can embrace failure as a regular part of their journey, because 'God is daily shaping them to be like him, and they aren't finished yet'.

*

Chapter 15

Friendships and peer pressure

Key questions: How do I help my child not to worry about fitting in at school? His friends have such an influence on him, and I think it's because he doesn't want to stand out. How do I help him have the confidence to be himself when peer pressure is telling him to fit in? How can I encourage my child to be confident in meeting new friends and being a Christian where he is?

We want our children to have flourishing friendships within their schools and clubs. As they grow, though, they are increasingly exposed to other people's influence, and we feel as if we have less and less time to combat the world's voice in their lives. How can we equip our children to be confident within their friendship groups? How can we equip them to be confident within the wider context of a non-Christian community that pressurises them to change to its standards?

A deeper look at the issue

Children can often feel powerless when it comes to friendships and interacting with the world confidently. From making friendships to coping with conflicts of values and behaviour, it is a tricky journey for our children to navigate.

When it comes to this issue, I'm reminded of whitewater rafting. When I was a child, my parents took me on a short, one-hour whitewater rafting trip in America. I was nine years old, and I was sure that this was the most dangerous thing I would ever do in my life. After we had waited in a short queue, the guides strapped a lifejacket on to me for the inevitable moment when I would be ejected from the raft into the churning water. They then handed me a paddle, crammed me and my parents into the raft with eight other people and set off with us, down the river. The guide called out which side of the raft we should paddle on and how hard, and we all tried our best. I'm fairly sure my paddle didn't even reach the water half of the time, but I remember watching the guides work incredibly hard at steering and paddling while we did our part. Our job was simply to listen to the men calling out instructions and to follow them well. If we all did that, we would emerge victorious and alive.

Many years later, on a trip with my husband, we too decided to go whitewater kayaking, but this time there would be only one person per kayak. My life was in my own hands. I was nervous. On the previous rafting trip, I had felt safe because the experts had been in my boat, directing the journey, doing most of the hard work and telling me what to do and when. How in the world was I going to handle it on my own?

My husband is an experienced kayaker, so, as soon as we got in the queue, he began to explain all the equipment— why the paddles are shaped the way they are, how to stroke smoothly and turn well, and where to position myself to be the most comfortable. After we had put on our waterproof gear, he showed me how kayaks are balanced and shaped, so that I could understand how to turn them. Once we were in the water, he encouraged me to paddle around while he coached me in the strokes. At first, we paddled in silence while I found my path in the river and tried to find the current. Before we came to the first set of rapids, Mark pulled up beside me and showed me the path he was going to take, the potentially tricky spots ahead, and how to face my kayak into the waves. Then he zoomed off and I was on my own to try. I faced down the waves and dug hard into the turns. I spun once, got stuck once, panicked slightly and figured how to get out. By the time I emerged on the other side of those first rapids, I felt triumphant.

Mark encouraged me as I chattered about my experience, and we went down the river again. For every new tricky bit, he would check to make sure I felt comfortable to navigate it well. He adjusted his briefings to include new information only just before I needed it, and so I continued, comfortably making mistakes and trying to apply all I was learning.

When our children are small, they are in our boat on the journey of life. We do most of the heavy lifting and we navigate the rapids for them. As they grow older, they can't stay in our boat any longer. They must grow in independence and must face the whitewaters of friendships and choices and opposition by themselves. They have to navigate on their own, making their mistakes and learning their lessons, but we can still coach them through the process beforehand. We can give them the skills they need to respond to the next section, to find the wisest path ahead, and to engage with life's rapids proactively, with confidence, handling mistakes and successes with joy and determination.

Helping our children to live confidently when we are not there is a large part of our calling. I feel it is essential that we are proactive in equipping our children's hearts and minds to be ready to respond to issues before they come up. If we wait until a crisis emerges, we will be for ever chasing our children as they toss aimlessly in the rapids; but if we can get ahead of potential problems and train our children to handle them well, they will feel ready to engage confidently with problems when they arise.

Above all, we encourage our children to 'throw off everything that hinders and the sin that so easily entangles. And... run with perseverance the race marked out for us, fixing our eyes on Jesus, the pioneer and perfecter of faith' (Hebrews 12:1–2). As our children navigate their race, we must remember that Jesus has gone on this path before us, and, as we coach our children, so will he, shaping them to be more and more like him.

Putting the 'hearts and minds' tools into action

Here are a few suggestions to get you started in building a core of confidence.

Building good friendships

- Hearts: Connect children to yourself and God; help them be powerful for the next time
- Minds: Direct attention and values; use foundational phrases; equip children to be powerful in shaping their own minds

When training our children to chart the course ahead of them, we need to teach them how to look for the safe paths, the beneficial places in which to journey. In the flow of relationships and opposition, they need to learn how to establish good friendships and how to operate in a healthy way with their friends.

A key pressure for many children is in finding new friends. Sometimes this is necessary because they are entering a new situation; other times it's because their existing friendship group isn't working for them any more and they need to branch out. Depending on our children's personalities, they may instinctively operate in a powerless or passive way. They can become stressed, hoping that someone will be their friend or just be nice to them and invite them to play. Making friends becomes a combination of chance and of being appealing enough to be chosen. Let's look again at our core of confidence:

> God is awesome and holy, and he loves me
> totally and unreasonably.
>
> He is daily shaping me to be like him, and I am
> not finished yet.
>
> I am invited to be a small part of his
> wonderful plans.

Who our children become in any situation doesn't depend on waiting to be chosen; it's about being a small part of God's plans, as imperfect and loved as they are.

Have a chat with your child, preparing her for a new situation. Describe how easy it is for all of us to think about ourselves when we are meeting new people, but help her to understand that God has brought her to this place and he has made her to be powerful in this situation with him. When she goes to school tomorrow, perhaps she could wonder with God, 'How are other people feeling? Who needs a friend? Who needs someone to sit with, laugh with and be encouraged by? Who needs to be defended or helped?'

Do some roleplay games about meeting new people. Help your child to think of questions to ask someone in order to start a conversation or invite them to participate in an activity. Pose scenarios for your child to solve: 'What would you do if a new child came into your class who didn't speak English? That's a tricky one! What do you think?' By doing this, children can think through possibilities in advance and have something to remember when the situation arises.

As you read books together, highlight the qualities of good and encouraging friendships within the stories. Look at the friendships and sibling relationships in the Bible, between Jonathan and David, Paul and Barnabas, Mary and Martha, Aaron and Moses, and so on. Give praise when your child is functioning as a good and faithful friend, and praise your children's friends when you hear stories of health in their relationship. Once, our son was punched at school. When we were debriefing him about the situation, he told us how his best friend had tried to stop the aggressive child from hurting him. As this friend had dived in the way to protect my son, he'd received a violent shove and a punch in the head for his efforts. But by doing that, he'd created the space for them both to escape.

Instead of choosing to focus on the altercation straight away, we ended up talking for a long time about how wonderful it was to have such a faithful friend, and what it means to be faithful to someone in friendship. We talked about sacrifice, and how Jesus said that true friendship means being willing to sacrifice ourselves for others (John 15:13), just as his friend did. When we finally went in to chat with his teacher, the incident itself was minor in his mind, but the joy of his friendship had increased.

Encourage your children to love their friends well. Facilitate their love languages. If they show love through making gifts, spending time, writing notes, giving hugs or doing nice things, create space for them to do so. The more powerful your children feel to invest in life-giving friendships, the more their core of confidence will grow.

Navigating the rapids

- Hearts: All tools
- Minds: All tools

Our children will often be among friends who do not know God. It is essential that we help them explore scenarios about what could happen out in the world, so that they will have a mental framework from which they can make decisions.

Talk to your children about control and manipulation and how some people like to be in charge of others. Explain that it happens a lot. Some people say, 'Do this or I won't be your friend' or, 'If you were my friend, you would do this with me' or even, 'You are stupid if you think that.' Some people think they can coerce others into doing things, but tell your children that you know that they are in charge of their own choices. Let them know that you will hold them accountable for their choices with their friends, both good and bad.

When you watch television programmes with them, pause and notice when a friend is behaving in a manipulative way, and give alternatives for the way healthy friendships should work or what the character in the programme could have done about it. Spot it when it happens at home and ask, for example, 'Wait a minute, are you trying to manipulate your dad? Are you trying to control him?' The more we identify different types of manipulation and control, the more able our children will be to spot them and choose not to respond to them.

As your children get older, the kinds of manipulation

may vary, but they still reflect the same process. I remember that, when I was eight, my mum told me about note passing in class and how students would try to get others to deliver notes for them so that they wouldn't risk getting in trouble themselves. She told me that I could just say 'no' and that my job at school wasn't to be someone else's postman. If they wanted to do something wrong and risky, they needed to take the risk themselves. Whereas before I'd felt conflicted when asked to pass notes, the next time it happened I confidently said 'no'. Eight years later, my mum told me that sometimes certain guys might try to manipulate girls by saying, 'If you won't have sex with me, then we can't continue our relationship.' It was awkward coming from my mum, but important to hear. Sure enough, the first time a guy tried that with me, I actually laughed in his face. I couldn't believe he'd said it.

Whatever our children's ages or stages, by preparing them for the idea that people may try to manipulate them, we help them gain wisdom and confidence in choosing to walk in their own path and not in others'.

Empower your children to ask themselves, 'What are God's purposes here and how can I follow him?' As you go about your days together, pray quickly, asking God to give you opportunities to bring his love into the places where you'll be going. Respond with compassion to the needs you see with friends and strangers. Live generously and kindly. As we model this sort of behaviour with our children, we equip them to enter different scenarios in the world, whether they are with their friends or not. They will see that God is doing things all around and is inviting us to make a difference with him. Through their experiences with you, they will be making opportunities for God's love to be powerful and will become aware of how they can sense God's presence and purposes in the everyday world.

Equip your children to know when to stay and when to leave. Sometimes people will be living without love at the centre of their lives. People's words hurt each other or their bodies hurt each other. People make unwise choices because they want others to like them, or they try to manipulate others to do what they want. Sometimes love means stepping in and not letting people hurt each other. Sometimes it means we protect people who have no voice or are being treated unfairly, and sometimes it means that we need to leave a situation. We need to be wise and leave when other people's choices could hurt or damage us, because that isn't right.

Create some tools for your children, so that they know how to leave well. This might involve just helping them work out how to walk away and play with someone else. As they get older, it might involve working with them on exit strategies for parties, or equipping them to choose wisely when to leave an activity, knowing that you are willing to come and fetch them. When our children feel equipped to walk away from a situation, it turns a scary moment of feeling cornered into a moment of freedom and choice.

We need to teach our children how to stick to God's values without forcing their values on others. Children often feel persecuted for their faith, not because they actually are, but because they haven't figured out how to live with their values among people who don't share the same ones. So they make mistakes, which cause other people to get angry. Children can end up defending their own values by attacking and judging their friends and arguing about what everyone 'should do'. Helping them to know how to explain their choices to others, and how to put love at the centre of their interaction with other people, means that they will hold firm to God's values without hurting others.

Have conversations with your child about how God wants every person to know that he loves them, and wants everyone to connect with him. We are all not finished yet, and we are on a journey of life with God as he loves us and transforms us. Other people don't have that wonderful relationship with God yet. It's not our job to judge other people and say, 'Hey, you aren't perfect yet!' Our job is just to be on our journey of love with God and to help people experience his love and see him well. It's OK if people don't understand our choices, just as it's OK if we don't understand theirs. What's most important is that love is at the centre of all our relationships, so that people can know God more and more.

Facing the opposition

- Hearts: All tools
- Minds: All tools

There will always be children and adults who are cruel in this world. We will never be able to protect our children from all the words and actions of every person at their school or in clubs, so equipping them to deal with criticism, rumours and bullying is an essential part of helping them be effective and peaceful in the world. Remember, parenting for confidence is not about creating perfect children who are able to resist all the temptations and effects of the world upon their lives. We aren't world-proofing our children. We are building a core within them that empowers them to meet the world head on, grapple with any fears and confidently, gracefully, wisely and powerfully engage with it.

It is always helpful to raise opposition as a possibility, not to scare them but to ensure that it isn't a surprise when it happens. When people get hurt, they get angry, and when they get angry they often try to hurt others. Sometimes we are in the path of that anger. It hurts. One day we'll live in a world with no hurt, but today is not that day.

When it happens to your child, ask questions to understand better how he or she is responding. In my experience, a child's hurt can be in response either to the words used or to the encounter in which someone deliberately sought to hurt him with words or actions. Ask questions to uncover your child's hurt and understand the root better. If we focus on the words, when his pain is really about the insecurity of having an angry person in his life, we won't be ministering the right truth, and vice versa. Words are strange things: the most ridiculous ones can hurt deeply. Remember to respond with empathy, as these are the moments in which your child needs to be understood and heard, even if he was called 'boogie face' and you think it's the silliest name in the world.

Coach your children in how to deal with the words that are designed to hurt them. Since my dad is a police officer, he naturally has to deal with a lot of verbal abuse from the people he serves. When I was very young, he taught me simply to ask the question 'Is that true?' Often, children are so busy being offended by someone who tries to hurt them with words that the words themselves stick in and begin to infect the way they think about themselves. Just like in the 'spot the lie' game that I described before, when a word or phrase is in our children's brains, we can train them to ask questions. 'Is that true? Am I really a boogie face? Of course not! That is ridiculous!' We can train them to picture the word being crumpled up and thrown into a bin in their head, never to be seen again. Nothing that isn't good and right and pure and true gets to stay in our brains.

There are circumstances when insults have a grain of truth in them, but they are equally easy to dismiss. When I was a child, a few people tried calling me 'four eyes' because I wore glasses. I remember telling them that I only had two eyes, obviously. My glasses were there to help me see and play sports better and get through school without headaches. But I'm not perfect and neither is my body. Get into the habit of asking questions for yourself and empowering your children to hold up insults and ask, 'Is that true? Is that true, based on what I see or on what you see as a parent?' Help your children to find the core of confidence that removes labels and simply empowers them to be loved by an awesome and wonderful God.

Investigate with your children how to handle conflict when it happens. Often, children are hurt and run directly to an adult for help or justice when they need assistance in achieving proper resolution. I encourage children to look at Matthew 18:15–17:

'If your brother or sister sins, go and point out their fault, just between the two of you. If they listen to you, you have won them over. But if they will not listen, take one or two others along, so that "every matter may be established by the testimony of two or three witnesses." If they still refuse to listen, tell it to the church; and if they refuse to listen even to the church, treat them as you would a pagan or a tax collector.'

Children often run to adults because they feel ill-equipped to deal with conflict directly. Assist your children in learning how to say, 'No, that hurts me' when it happens, or 'I don't like you saying that to me. It's not nice. No, thank you.' The more they feel released in the moment to confront what they don't like in relationships, the better able they will be to deal with situations as they arise, instead of bottling them up. If the aggressive person doesn't adjust his behaviour, then by all means the child can bring someone else in—an adult, if they wish. If the offender still doesn't change, scripture says that we are to deal with them as if they were 'a Gentile or tax collector', which generally means someone who is set apart from you, no longer a close friend but an outsider. Essentially, if a friend is not safe to be around and is not willing to change his behaviour, we need to adjust the level of trust we have with that person and move a bit further away.

Hurt will almost always lead to an issue of forgiveness. For children, forgiveness can be confusing, as they will often equate forgiveness with a lack of justice or a need to put themselves back into an unsafe place. As we discuss forgiveness with them, we will need to explain it well. Jesus doesn't give us an option on forgiveness: we have been forgiven and so we are to forgive others. Often, this topic is best approached as part of a heart conversation, after you have really understood what your children are feeling and you have affirmed their emotions.

I often tell children that hanging on to our anger and hurt makes us want to punish the other person ourselves, to see them punished so that we feel better. But that's God's job, not ours. He is in charge of justice; my job is to love. Forgiving means deciding that I'm going to let God be in charge of the other person. I choose not to spend time thinking about that other person with an angry heart. Instead I tell God how I feel and ask him to heal my heart, and I put the other person in God's hands to deal with as he wants. We can talk with our children about beginning these conversations with God, if they want to, or we can lay the foundation by describing forgiveness so that they can do it on their own later.

Friendships are one of our greatest gifts from God, and, as we see our children grow in healthy relationships and deal with difficult complications, we can rejoice that they know how to face challenges with the peace that comes from a core of confidence in God.

*

Conclusion

Parenting is a long and arduous journey. It is also one of the greatest privileges of our lives.

Please take this book as a set of tools in your parenting box. Do not feel that you now need to use all of them in every moment. Trust that God will direct you to use different tools at different times.

Remember that you are not alone on this great journey. As you partner with God to parent your children, I believe that you will joyfully see the fruit of God in their lives. I pray that you will daily feel confident that the God who made you, who called you to parent these children, will fill you with his wisdom, his strength and his voice.

If you want any free resources or encouragements, please go to www.rachelturner.org.uk and sign up for regular communications, tips, videos and ideas to support you in parenting your children for faith, purpose and confidence.

May the God who makes all things possible bless you with terrific sleep, hope and dreams for your children's tomorrows, and a clear and peaceful heart, that you may walk through this season of your life with deep joy and greater sense of his closeness.